Book 6

MAXIMIZE YOUR POTENTIAL

THROUGH THE POWER OF YOUR

SUBCONSCIOUS MIND

FOR AN

Enriched Life

Other Hay House Classics Titles by Dr. Joseph Murphy

Believe in Yourself
Miracles of Your Mind
Techniques in Prayer Therapy

Other Books in the MAXIMIZE YOUR POTENTIAL Series:

Book 1: *Maximize Your Potential Through the*
Power of Your Subconscious Mind to Overcome Fear and Worry

—·—

Book 2: *Maximize Your Potential Through the*
Power of Your Subconscious Mind to Create Wealth and Success

—·—

Book 3: *Maximize Your Potential Through the Power of Your*
Subconscious Mind to Develop Self-Confidence and Self-Esteem

—·—

Book 4: *Maximize Your Potential Through the*
Power of Your Subconscious Mind for Health and Vitality

—·—

Book 5: *Maximize Your Potential Through the*
Power of Your Subconscious Mind for a More Spiritual Life

—·—

All of the above are available at your local bookstore,
or may be ordered by visiting:

Hay House USA: **www.hayhouse.com**®
Hay House Australia: **www.hayhouse.com.au**
Hay House UK: **www.hayhouse.co.uk**
Hay House South Africa: **www.hayhouse.co.za**
Hay House India: **www.hayhouse.co.in**

Book 6

MAXIMIZE YOUR POTENTIAL

THROUGH THE POWER OF YOUR

SUBCONSCIOUS MIND

FOR AN

Enriched Life

One of a Series of Six Books
by
Dr. Joseph Murphy

Edited and Updated for the 21st Century
by Arthur R. Pell, Ph.D.

HAY HOUSE, INC.
Carlsbad, California • New York City
London • Sydney • Johannesburg
Vancouver • Hong Kong • New Delhi

DR. JOSEPH MURPHY

Maximize Your Potential Through the Power of Your Subconscious Mind for an Enriched Life is one of a series of six books by Joseph Murphy, D.D., Ph.D., edited and updated for the 21st century by Arthur R. Pell, Ph.D. Copyright © 2005 The James A. Boyer Revocable Trust. Exclusive worldwide rights in all languages available only through JMW Group Inc.

Published and distributed in the United States by: Hay House, Inc.: www.hayhouse. com • **Published and distributed in Australia by:** Hay House Australia Pty. Ltd.: www.hayhouse.com.au • **Published and distributed in the United Kingdom by:** Hay House UK, Ltd.: www.hayhouse.co.uk • **Published and distributed in the Republic of South Africa by:** Hay House SA (Pty), Ltd.: www.hayhouse.co.za • **Distributed in Canada by:** Raincoast: www.raincoast.com • **Published in India by:** Hay House Publishers India: www.hayhouse.co.in

Design: Riann Bender

Library of Congress Cataloging-in-Publication Data

Murphy, Joseph, 1898–1981.
  Maximize your potential through the power of your subconscious mind for an enriched life : one of a series of six books / by Joseph Murphy ; edited and updated for the 21st century by Arthur R. Pell. -- 1st Hay House ed.
    p. cm.
  "Book 6."
  ISBN 978-1-4019-1219-2 (tradepaper)
  1. New Thought. I. Pell, Arthur R. II. Title.
  BF639.M8312 2008
  154.2--dc22   2006100770

ISBN: 978-1-4019-1219-2

11 10 09 08   4 3 2 1
1st Hay House edition, December 2008

Printed in the United States of America

CONTENTS

———·•·———

Introduction to the Series vii

Preface xix

Chapter 1: The Wonders of Master Thought 1

Chapter 2: Your Friend, the Subconscious 17

Chapter 3: The Unbelievable Power of Suggestion 33

Chapter 4: Practical Meditation 49

Chapter 5: Do the Constellations Govern You? 63

Chapter 6: *Speaking in Tongues:* What It Really Means 73

Chapter 7: A New Look at Reincarnation 87

Chapter 8: Living an Inspired Life 103

Chapter 9: Getting Results from Prayer 121

Chapter 10: How to Think with Authority 131

Biography of Joseph Murphy 145

Introduction to the Series

*W*ake up and live! No one is destined to be unhappy or consumed with fear and worry, live in poverty, suffer ill health, and feel rejected and inferior. God created all humans in His image and has given us the power to overcome adversity and attain happiness, harmony, health, and prosperity.

You have within you the power to enrich your life! How to do this is no secret. It has been preached, written about, and practiced for millennia. You will find it in the works of the ancient philosophers, and all of the great religions have preached it. It is in the Hebrew scriptures, the Christian Gospels, Greek philosophy, the Muslim Koran, the Buddhist sutras, the Hindu Bhagavad Gita, and the writings of Confucius and Lao Tse. You will find it in the works of modern psychologists and theologians.

This is the basis of the philosophy of Dr. Joseph Murphy, one of the great inspirational writers and lecturers of the 20th century. He was not just a clergyman, but also a major figure in the modern interpretation of scriptures and other religious writings. As minister-director of the Church of Divine Science in Los Angeles, his lectures and sermons were attended by 1,300 to 1,500 people every Sunday, and millions tuned in to his daily radio program. He wrote more than 30 books, and his most well-known one, *The Power of the Unconscious Mind,* was first published in 1963 and became an immediate bestseller. It was acclaimed as one of the greatest self-help guides ever written. Millions of copies have, and continue to be, sold all over the world.

Following the success of this book, Dr. Murphy lectured to audiences of thousands in several countries. In his lectures he pointed out how real people have radically improved their lives by applying specific aspects of his concepts, and he provided practical guidelines on how all people can enrich themselves.

Dr. Murphy was a proponent of the New Thought movement, which was developed in the late 19th and early 20th century by many philosophers and deep thinkers who studied it and preached, wrote, and practiced a new way of looking at life. By combining metaphysical, spiritual, and pragmatic approaches to the way we think and live, they uncovered the secret for attaining what we truly desire.

This philosophy wasn't a religion in the traditional sense, but it was based on an unconditional belief in a higher being, an eternal presence: God. It was called by various names, such as "New Thought" and "New Civilization."

The proponents of New Thought or New Civilization preached a fresh idea of life that makes use of methods that lead to perfected results. They based their thinking on the concept that the human soul is connected with the atomic mind of universal substance, which links our lives with the universal law of supply, and we have the power to use it to enrich our lives. To achieve our goals, we must work, and through this working, we may suffer the thorns and heartaches of humankind. We can do all these things only as we have found the law and worked out an understanding of the principles that God seemed to have written in riddles in the past.

The New Thought concept can be summed up in these words:

You can become what you want to be.

All that we achieve and all that we fail to achieve is the direct result of our own thoughts. In a just and ordered universe, where loss of balance would mean total destruction, individual responsibility must be absolute. Our weaknesses, strengths, purity, and impurity are ours alone. They are brought about by ourselves and not by another. They can only be altered by ourselves, and never by anyone else. All of our happiness and suffering evolve from within. As we think, so we are; as we continue to think, so we remain. The only way we can rise, conquer, and achieve is by lifting up our thoughts. The only reason we may remain weak, abject, and miserable is to *refuse* to elevate our minds.

All achievements—whether in the business, intellectual, or spiritual world—are the result of definitely directed thought; and are governed by the same law and are reached by the same method. The only difference lies in the object of attainment. Those who would accomplish little must sacrifice little; those who would achieve much must sacrifice much; those who would attain a great deal must sacrifice a great deal.

New Thought means a new life: a way of living that is healthier, happier, and more fulfilling in every possible manner and expression.

Actually, there is nothing new in this, for it is as old and time-honored as humankind. It is novel to us when we discover the truths of life that set us free from lack, limitation, and unhappiness. At that moment, New Thought becomes a recurring, expanding awareness of the creative power within; of mind-principle; and of our Divine potential to be, to do, and to express more of our individual and natural abilities, aptitudes, and talents. The central mind-principle is that new thoughts, ideas, attitudes, and beliefs create new conditions. According to our beliefs, is it done unto us— good, bad, or indifferent. The essence of New Thought consists of the continual renewing of our mind, that we may manifest what is good, acceptable, and the perfect will of God.

To prove is to know surely, and to have trustworthy knowledge and experience. The truths of New Thought are practical, easy to demonstrate, and within the realm of accomplishment of everyone—if and when he or she chooses. All that is required is an open mind and a willing heart: open to hearing old truths presented in a different way; willing to change and to relinquish outmoded beliefs and to accept unfamiliar ideas and concepts—to have a higher vision of life, or a healing presence within.

The rebirth of our mind constitutes the entire purpose and practice of New Thought. Without this ongoing daily renewal, there can be no change. New Thought establishes and realizes an entirely new attitude and consciousness that inspires and enables us to enter into "life more abundant."

We have within us limitless powers to choose and to decide, and complete freedom to be conformed or to be transformed. To be conformed is to live according to that which already has taken or been given form—that which is visible and apparent to our own senses, including the ideas, opinions, beliefs, and edicts of others. It is to live and to be governed "by the fleeting and unstable fashions and conditions of the moment." The very word *conformed* suggests that our present environment has shape, and that we do not and should not deny its existence. All around us there are injustices, improprieties, and inequalities. We may and do find ourselves involved in them at times, and we should face them with courage and honesty and do our best to resolve them with the integrity and intelligence that we now possess.

Generally, the world accepts and believes that our environment is the cause of our present condition and circumstance—and the usual reaction and tendency is to drift into a state of acquiescence and quiet acceptance of the present. This is conformity of the worst kind: the consciousness of defeatism. It's worse because it is self-imposed. It is giving all power and attention to the outer, manifested state. New Thought insists on the renewal of the mind, and the recognition and acknowledgment of our responsibility in life—our ability to respond to the truths we now know.

One of the most active and effective of New Thought teachers, Charles Fillmore, co-founder of the Unity School of Christianity, was a firm believer in personal responsibility. In his book *The Revealing Word,* he wrote (simply, and without equivocation): "Our consciousness is our real environment. The outer environment is always in correspondence to our consciousness."

Anyone who is open and willing to accept the responsibility has begun the transformation—the renewal of the mind that enables us to participate in our transformed life. "To transform" is "to change from one condition or state to another" (which is qualitatively better and more fulfilling) "from lack to abundance; loneliness to companionship; limitation to fullness; illness to vibrant health"—through this indwelling wisdom and power, the healing presence will remain within.

True and granted, there are some things we cannot change: the movement of the planets, the turn of the seasons, the pull of the oceans and tides, and the apparent rising and setting of the sun. Neither can we alter the minds and thoughts of another person—but we can change ourselves.

Who can prevent or inhibit the movement of your imagination and will? Only you can give that power to another. You can be transformed by the renewing of your mind. This is the key to a new life. You're a recording machine; and all the beliefs, impressions, opinions, and ideas accepted by you are impressed in your deeper subconscious. But you can change. You can begin now to fill your mind with noble and Godlike patterns of thoughts, and align yourself with the infinite spirit within. Claim beauty, love, peace, wisdom, creative ideas . . . and the infinite will respond accordingly, transforming your mind, body, and circumstances. Your thought is the medium between your spirit, your body, and the material world.

The transformation begins as we meditate, think upon, and absorb into our mentality those qualities that we desire to experience and express. Theoretical knowledge is good and necessary. We should understand what we're doing and why. However, actual change depends entirely on stirring up the gifts within—the invisible and intangible spiritual power given fully to every one of us.

This, and only this, ultimately breaks up and dissolves the very real claims and bondage of past unhappiness and distress. In addition, it heals the wounds of heartbreak and emotional pain. We all desire and require peace of mind—the greatest gift—in order to bring it into our environment. Mentally and emotionally, contemplate Divine peace, filling our mind and heart, our entire being. First say, "Peace be unto this house."

To contemplate lack of peace, disharmony, unhappiness, and discord, and expect peace to manifest is to expect the apple seed to grow into a pear. It makes little or no sense, and it violates all sense of reason, but it is the way of the world. We must seek ways to change our minds—to repent where necessary. As a result, renewal will occur, following naturally. It is desirable and necessary to transform our lives by ceasing to conform to the world's way of choosing or deciding, according to the events already formed and manifested.

The word *metaphysical* has become a synonym for the modern, organized movement. It was first used by Aristotle. Considered by some to have been his greatest writing, his 13th volume was simply entitled *Metaphysics*. The dictionary definition is: "Beyond natural science; the science of pure being." *Meta-* means "above, or beyond." *Metaphysics,* then, means "above or beyond physics"— "above or beyond the physical," the world of form. "Meta" is above that; it is the spirit of the mind, which is behind all things.

Biblically, the spirit of God is good. "They that worship God worship the spirit, or truth." When we have the spirit of goodness, truth, beauty, love, and goodwill, it is actually the Divine in us, moving through us. God, truth, life, energy, spirit—can it not be defined? How can it be? "To define it is to limit it."

This is expressed in a beautiful old meditation:

Ever the same in my innermost being: eternal, absolutely one, whole, complete, perfect; I AM indivisible, timeless, shapeless, ageless—without face, form, or figure. I AM the silent brooding presence, fixed in the hearts of all men (and women).

We must believe and accept that whatever we imagine and feel to be true will come to pass; whatever we desire for another, we are wishing for ourselves.

Emerson wrote: "We become what we think about all day long." In other words and most simply stated: Spirit, thought, mind, and meta is the expression of creative presence and power—and as in nature (physical laws), any force can be used two ways. For example, water can clean us or drown us; electricity can make life easier or more deadly. The Bible says: "I form the light, and create darkness; I make peace, and evil; I, the Lord, do all these things—I wound, I heal; I bless, I curse."

No angry deity is punishing us; we punish ourselves by misuse of the mind. We also are blessed (benefited) when we comprehend this fundamental principle and presence, and learn and accept a new thought or an entire concept.

Metaphysics, then, is the study of causation—concerned not with the effect that is now manifest, but rather with that which is causing the result. This discipline approaches spiritual ideas as scientists approach the world of form, just as they investigate the mind or causation from which the visible is formed, or derived. If a mind is changed, or a cause is changed, the effect is changed.

The strength and beauty of metaphysics, in my opinion, is that it is not confined to any one particular creed, but is universal. One can be a Jew, Christian, Muslim, or Buddhist and yet still be a metaphysician.

There are poets, scientists, and philosophers who claim no creed; their belief is metaphysical.

Jesus was a master metaphysician—he understood the mind and employed it to lift up, inspire, and heal others.

When Mahatma Gandhi (the "great-souled" one) was asked what his religion was, he replied, "I am a Christian . . . a Jew . . . a Buddhist . . . a Hindu . . . I AM all these things."

The term *New Thought* has become a popular, generalized term. Composed of a very large number of churches, centers, prayer groups, and institutions, this has become a metaphysical movement that reveals the oneness or unity of humankind with infinite life . . . with the innate dignity, worth, or value of every individual. In fact, and in truth, the emphasis is on the individual rather than on an organizational body or function. But as mentioned, there is nothing new in New Thought. Metaphysics is actually the oldest of all religious approaches. It reveals our purpose to express God, and the greater measures of the Good: "I AM come to bring you life and that more abundantly." It reveals our identity: "children of the infinite" who are loved and have spiritual value as necessary parts of the Creative Holy (whole) One.

Metaphysics enables and assists us to return to our Divine Source, and ends the sense of separation and feeling of alienation; of wandering in a barren, unfriendly desert wasteland. This approach has always been, is now, and ever will be available to all—patiently waiting our discovery and revelation.

Many thousands have been introduced to New Thought through one or another of its advocates. Its formation was gradual, and usually considered to have begun with Phineas P. Quimby. In a fascinating article in *New Thought* magazine, Quimby wrote about his work in 1837. After experimenting with mesmerism for a period of years, he concluded that it was not the hypnotism itself, but the conditioning of the subconscious, which led to the resulting changes. Although Quimby had very little formal education, he had a brilliant, investigative mind and was an original thinker. In addition, he was a prolific writer and diarist. Records have been published detailing the development of his findings. He eventually became a wonderful student of the Bible and duplicated two-thirds of the Old and New Testament healings. He found that there was much confusion about the true meaning of many biblical passages, which caused misunderstanding and misinterpretation of Jesus Christ.

All through the 20th century, so many inspired teachers, authors, ministers, and lecturers contributed to the New Thought movement. Dr. Charles E. Braden, of the University of Chicago, called these people "spirits in rebellion" because these men and women were truly breaking free from existing dogmatism, rituals, and creeds. (Rebelling at inconsistencies in the old traditions led some individuals to fear religion.) Dr. Braden became discontent with the status quo and refused to conform any longer.

New Thought is an individual practice of the truths of life—a gradual, continuing process. We can learn a bit today, and even more tomorrow. Never will we experience a point where there is nothing more to be discovered. It is infinite, boundless, and eternal. We have all the time we need—eternity. Many of us are impatient with ourselves, and with what we consider our failures. Looking back, though, we discover that these have been periods of learning, and we needn't make these mistakes again. Progress may seem ever so slow: "In patience, possess ye your soul."

In Dr. Murphy's book *Pray Your Way Through It: The Revelation,* he commented that heaven was noted as being "awareness," and Earth, "manifestation." Your new heaven is your revised point of view—your new dimension of consciousness. When we see—that is, see spiritually, we then realize that in the absolute, all is blessed harmony, boundless love, wisdom, complete peace, and perfection. Identify with these truths, calm the sea of fear; have confidence and faith, and become stronger and surer.

In the books in this series, Dr. Murphy has synthesized the profundities of this power and has put them into an easily under-stood and pragmatic form so that you can apply them immediately to your life. As Dr. Murphy was a Protestant minister, many of his examples and citations come from the Bible. The concepts these passages illustrate should not be viewed as sectarian. Indeed, their messages are universal and are preached in most religions and phi-losophies. He often reiterated that the essence of knowledge is in the law of life and belief. It is not Catholic, Protestant, Muslim, or Hindu; it is pure and simple faith: "Do unto others accordingly."

Dr. Murphy's wife, Dr. Jean Murphy, continued his ministry after his death in 1981. In a lecture she gave in 1986, quoting her late husband, she reiterated his philosophy:

> I want to teach men and women of their Divine Origin, and the powers regnant within them. I want to inform them that this power is within and that they are their own saviors and capable of achieving their own salvation. This is the message of the Bible, and nine-tenths of our confusion today is due to wrongful, literal interpretation of the life-transforming truths offered in it.
>
> I want to reach the majority, the man on the street, the woman overburdened with duty and suppression of her talents and abilities. I want to help others at every stage or level of consciousness to learn of the wonders within.

She said of her husband: "He was a practical mystic, possessed by the intellect of a scholar, the mind of a successful executive, the heart of the poet." His message summed up was: "You are the king, the ruler of your world, for you are one with God."

Joseph Murphy was a firm believer that it was God's plan for people to be healthy, prosperous, and happy. He countered those theologians and others who claimed that desire is evil and urged people to crush it. He said that extinction of our longings means apathy—no feeling, no action. He preached that desire is a gift of God. It is healthy and wholesome to want to become more and better than we were yesterday . . . in the areas of health, abundance, companionship, security, and more. How could these be wrong?

Desire is behind all progress. Without it, nothing would be accomplished. It is the creative power and must be channeled constructively. For example, if one is poor, yearning for wealth wells up from within; if one is ill, there is a wish for health; if lonely, there is a desire for companionship and love.

We must believe that we can improve our lives. A belief—whether it is true, false, or merely indifferent—sustained over a period of time becomes assimilated and is incorporated into our mentality. Unless countermanded by faith of an opposite nature, sooner or later it takes form and is expressed or experienced as fact, form, condition, circumstance, and the events of life. We have the power within us to change negative beliefs to positive ones, and thereby change ourselves for the better.

You give the command and your subconscious mind will faithfully obey it. You will get a reaction or response according to the nature of the thought you hold in your conscious mind. Psychologists and psychiatrists point out that when thoughts are conveyed to your subconscious mind, impressions are made in your brain cells. As soon as this part of you accepts any idea, it proceeds to put it into effect immediately. It works by association of ideas and uses every bit of knowledge that you have gathered in your lifetime to bring about its purpose. It draws on the infinite power, energy, and wisdom within you, lining up all the laws of nature to get its way. Sometimes it seems to bring about an immediate solution to your difficulties, but at other times it may take days, weeks, or longer.

The habitual thinking of your conscious mind establishes deep grooves in your subconscious mind. This is very favorable for you if your recurring thoughts are harmonious, peaceful, and constructive. On the other hand, if you have indulged in fear, worry, and other destructive concepts, the remedy is to recognize the omnipotence of your subconscious and decree freedom, happiness, perfect health, and prosperity. Your subconscious mind, being creative and one with your Divine source, will proceed to create the freedom and happiness that you have earnestly declared.

Now for the first time, Dr. Murphy's lectures have been combined, edited, and updated in six new books that bring his teachings into the 21st century. To enhance and augment this original text, we have incorporated material from some of Jean Murphy's lectures and have added examples of people whose success reflects Dr. Murphy's philosophy.

The other works in this series are listed on the second page of this book, but just reading them will not improve your state of being. To truly maximize your potential, you must study these principles, take them to heart, integrate them into your mentality, and apply them as an integral part of your approach to every aspect of your life.

— **Arthur R. Pell, Ph.D.**, editor

═╬═ ═╬═

Editor's Note: While updating these works, at times I have added current examples (that is, events and situations that may have occurred after Joseph Murphy's death) showing how basic principles presented by the author are still valid.

Preface

*L*iving an enriched life! Isn't that a goal all people aim for? In this book, Dr. Murphy shares his formula for achieving this universal dream. He presents time-tested ideas that all readers can apply to their personal lives.

As in all of his writings, Dr. Murphy draws on the Bible as the major source for his concepts. However, as a minister of The Church of Divine Science, his interpretation of the Judeo-Christian Bible is often quite different from that of traditional theologians. To understand his views, it's helpful to understand the basic philosophy of Divine Science, which is based on the belief in the omnipresence of God. Divine Science stresses that God isn't a physical person in the sky, for that perspective limits our ability to perceive His true nature. On the contrary, God is Spirit and is present in all things everywhere.

As part of the New Thought movement, Divine Science is an extremely positive approach that seeks to accept the good in people and in all of life, while denying the existence of any power or presence opposed to God. This religious philosophy acknowledges that there are evil appearances and suffering in the world, but ascribes these to our ignorance and erroneous use of God's laws of life.

Divine Science doesn't emphasize the sins of our past or the "future life," but instead focuses on the good that exists in all of us and what we can do right now to transform ourselves and our lives. Divine Science also believes in life eternal and considers the present moment as part of this infinite existence.

In the view of Divine Science, the mind is our connecting link with God or Divine Mind. It emphasizes that our every thought, feeling, and word affects our life. In addition, prayer isn't seen as a technique for changing God but as a way to expand and transform our mind—which will in turn change us.

As a Christian denomination, Divine Science proclaims the divinity of Jesus, but goes further and asserts that all people are children of God and are therefore Divine in nature. Jesus expressed His Divine potential and sought to show us how to express ours as well. Salvation is the expanding understanding of our innate Divinity and perfectibility through living life as modeled by Jesus.

From the perspective of Divine Science, the various religions are like spokes on a wheel whose hub is God. They may have different beliefs and approaches, but they're all seeking the one God; and they each contain good. Many of the precepts of Divine Science are accepted by non-Christians. Indeed, you'll find similar teachings in Buddhist writings, the Koran, the Talmud, and the works of philosophers from many cultures.

Dr. Murphy asks you to keep an open mind and not let your preconceptions and prejudices prevent you from studying, understanding, and applying the concepts presented in this book. If you absorb these truths, you'll maximize your potential through the power of your subconscious mind and achieve an enriched life.

— **Arthur R. Pell, Ph.D.**, editor

Chapter One

The Wonders of Master Thought

*M*any live miserable lives because of their disabilities—some perceived and others real. However, you can live an enriched and happy life only if you're determined to do so. An abundance of evidence shows that if you master your thoughts, you can create a wonderful existence. There are countless examples of how thoughts can be controlled so that the idea of disease or depression is eliminated from the subconscious. For example, a woman in New Hampshire who'd been confined to bed for years as a helpless and hopeless invalid was awakened in the middle of the night by flames in her room. The house was on fire, and there was no time for her to debate the question of whether she could rise and walk. The all-absorbing thought of impending danger erased the idea of disease from her mind, and she ran outside to safety. In her case, the cure was permanent.

As another illustration, my older brother, who was disabled by the severing of the large ligaments of his right ankle, couldn't set his foot on the floor during his waking hours because of the pain. Yet in his sleep, he would walk and go where he wanted to. In his somnambulant state, he forgot both his lameness and his body. The inner and real person walked, and the passive body accompanied him.

These cases aren't miracles, but examples of the harmony of the law of God—the sovereignty of the mind over the body.

⹌✦⹌

In a speech made many years ago in New York, Louis Kossuth, a former political leader of Hungary, said that many times he'd been confined to his bed because of illness. However, when he'd receive news from the army that demanded he take action, he'd say to his body, "Be well!" and it obeyed him.

He wasn't relying on sheer despotic willpower, which is as useless as trying to issue orders to a rock or a fly. No, Kossuth was acting on faith—the same faith that has subdued kingdoms, delivered justice, stopped the mouths of lions, and quenched fires.

People often ask, "How am I to get this faith?" The premise of this question is wrong. You aren't here to *get* faith in any way; you're here to *use* it. You're looking for what you already possess.

⹌✦⹌

A woman living in Los Angeles received a phone call from a man in New York City who arranged for her to meet with him to sign a contract for a lucrative deal. As she was absolutely sure she'd get this contract, she immediately flew to New York. However, when she got there the next day, she learned that he'd died in his sleep the night before. Rather than curse her bad luck, she used the master law and affirmed, "Infinite Spirit reveals the perfect plan for the development of my idea and a new contract in Its own way."

In time, she received an offer in Los Angeles that was far better than the one she would have had in New York.

⹌✦⹌

I was recently a guest at a wedding. We waited for about an hour, and the prospective bridegroom never showed up. Then word came to us that he'd died in the taxi on the way to the marriage ceremony. Now, the bride-to-be, Anne, wasn't the least bit disturbed. She said, "Well, I've been praying for guidance and right action. He must have reached the point of transition. God's love fills his soul, and His peace floods his mind."

She found out something interesting shortly afterward: Her fiancé had been an alcoholic and had also suffered from cardiovascular disease, but he hadn't revealed these things to her. You see, Anne had had the right attitude in focusing on receiving God's guidance. Her Higher Self protected her, and she was grateful. She was saved from a life with a troubled man, and she blessed him and walked on.

Three men who are equally good actors want to win the role of Romeo in Shakespeare's play. They can all play the part well, but only one of them can get the job. The actor who knows the law of mind affirms, "I successfully play the role of Romeo." Then he adds, "This or something grander or greater in the sight of my Higher Self easily unfolds for me." He doesn't lose touch with that master thought and isn't tense or anxious about whether his prayer will be answered, for he's confident it will be.

You know that the sun will rise in the morning and that the seeds you put into the soil will grow. You should also know that when you call upon Him, He answers you. It's impossible for your prayer to fail, so you're not the least bit worried. Either you'll get what you request or you'll receive something greater.

You must believe the biblical phrase "After you have done every-thing you can, you will be standing." Let's say that you've made your best effort to solve your problem. You've asked your friends and associates for help and have tried in every possible way to come up with a solution . . . but you haven't been able to. What are you going to do? Run around in circles? Complain about it to others?

What you need is peace of mind. Stop trying to solve your troubles with your conscious mind. Relax and sit quietly. *Be still and know that I am God.* Still the wheels of your mind and know that your own *I am* is the Lord God Almighty. It's the All-Wise, Eternal One. Get out of your own way, let the creative power of your subconscious mind take over, and it will provide the perfect answer for you. As Emerson wrote: "Let us take our bloated nothingness out of the path of the divine circuits."

Einstein also realized that the kingdom of God is within and that the realm of Divine Intelligence, Wisdom, and Power is in our own subconscious. After he'd tried to solve a problem with his conscious mind, asked his associates for help, and considered it from all angles, if he was still flummoxed he'd turn the challenge over to his deeper mind. Then he'd take a stroll on campus or have a cup of tea; and when he wasn't thinking about the problem at all, the answer would flow into his conscious mind like bread pops out of a toaster—it would well up from the depths. That's called the *incubation process.* The subconscious accepted his desire for a solution, and the answer was presented full-blown into his conscious mind. You can always tell when you've turned something over to the Infinite Intelligence because you're full of faith and confidence, you're relaxed, and you're not wondering *how? when?* and *where?* You've surrendered it to your deeper mind, which knows all.

A man asked me, "Why do I make so many mistakes?" The answer was that he was constantly telling himself, "I'm always messing up." As the tendency of the subconscious is to manifest our thoughts, he was causing himself many problems.

Psychiatrists say that the most powerful aspect of human nature is the unconscious, which we call the *subconscious*. If the subconscious is wrongly directed, it destroys our peace of mind and our effectiveness in this world. People who fail constantly have a pattern of failure. They have a sense of guilt and feel that they shouldn't succeed. They're driven by a deep, unconscious impulse. Many have a desire to hurt themselves—like the chronic gambler or alcoholic—because they want to atone for their guilt. However, no one is condemning them but themselves.

The Infinite Life Principle can't punish you. Its eyes are too pure to behold inequity. In the Bible, Jesus says: "Neither do I condemn thee: go, and sin no more." The Spirit within never criticizes—all judgment is given to the "son," which is your own mind.

At the International New Thought Convention in Chicago, I talked with Richard L., a minister who told me that at one time he'd been a pharmacist. He said, "I didn't want to be a pharmacist and hated everything about the profession, but my father, who was a pharmacist, insisted. He sent me to college and wanted me to take over his business when he retired. To please him, I went through the motions, but I resented the whole thing."

Richard explained that when he graduated, he took a job at another pharmacy. One day, he was dispensing a prescription for a quarter grain of codeine for a young girl. The custom in most

pharmacies is for a second pharmacist to double-check each prescription to make sure it's filled correctly. It turns out that in this
instance, Richard had mistakenly filled an order for cocaine rather
than for codeine. He said, "I was shocked at my error because it
would have been disastrous." Of course, the prescription was never
sent out, but he was fired from his position.

Richard said that he was so shocked that he went to see a psy-
chiatrist, who explained how he could have made such a grave
error. She said, "You hated the pharmaceutical business. Your father
more or less forced you into it against your will. You were always
saying, 'I hate this job. I want to get out of it. How can I move
on?'"

She told him bluntly that he'd wanted to leave his profession
and that his subconscious had therefore caused him to make a
mistake that would lead to his dismissal.

The subconscious always has a tendency to help us out. Today,
Richard is a very successful minister and is doing what he loves
instead of what his father wanted him to do.

A few years ago, I talked with a young lady who was 19 years
old. Her mother had passed on and left her a large sum of money
for her education, but her father told her, "You need to stay home
and take care of me. I'm old, and look at all I've done for you."
That's emotional blackmail. The dad was a querulous, demand-
ing old man. If he'd been loving, he would have rejoiced that his
daughter wanted an education and her own social life and apartment. Love always frees and gives; it doesn't say, "You have to stay
home with me." That's the opposite of love.

The daughter remained with her father out of a sense of duty
and waited on him three times a day, resenting every moment. She
wanted to leave but felt guilty because she knew that it was wrong
to hate her father. However, her subconscious came to her aid; she

cut her right hand severely, it became infected, and she was in the hospital for many weeks.

In talking with her, I said, "Hurting your hand wasn't an accident—there *are* no accidents. You had a basic desire to injure yourself to get out of an intolerable situation, and you programmed your subconscious by thinking, *I hate this and want to get out of here.* Your subconscious came to your aid in the wrong way because if you have negative, destructive emotions, it can't manifest in a constructive manner."

She'd impressed a highly destructive master thought on her subconscious, so I said, "All right, fill your mind now with the truths of God. Deliberately and continuously fill your subconscious with harmony, health, and peace by praying in the right way. But first empty your mind of all preconceived notions and misconceptions. Say, 'I forgive myself for harboring these negative, destructive thoughts. I release my father to God. I didn't create him, but I am responsible for the way I think about him. I release him and let him go.'"

Then she wrote a letter to her father that said: "Dad, you have plenty of money and can get yourself an aide. I'm going to college. Mom gave me money for a good education, and that's what I want. I love you but am no longer going to remain frustrated and unhappy at home. I wish for you all the blessings of life."

She affirmed, "I am a channel for the Divine. The truth flows through me, and I know what to do. I am always Divinely guided. I believe absolutely that I will always take the right road, for the Bible says: 'I will bring the blind by a way they did not know; I will lead them in paths they have not known.'"

As she repeated this prayer, her infection cleared up quickly, and she experienced a complete healing. God revealed the perfect plan for freedom, peace, and love.

Everything in the universe changes, and there's nothing we can do about it. Maybe we wake up in the morning and find out that there's a new president or king or a revolution somewhere. Nothing is forever, and everything passes away. However, there *is* something we can do about our attitude toward these constant changes: We can be in charge of our reactions to all that happens.

Lisa T. came to see me complaining that her co-workers were jealous of her. I said, "That's *their* problem, not yours. They're convinced that you're going to get all of the good things of life—that you'll be promoted, maybe marry the president of the company, and get many jewels. You just bless them and walk on. Jealousy is the green-eyed monster, the injured lover's hell, and the child of fear. It has nothing to do with you. You're not responsible if a thousand women are jealous of you."

A few years ago, Carol told me that some of her relatives had alleged that she'd hypnotized her father to compel him to bequeath everything to her in his will. They were taking her to court. She said, "The reason my dad left me everything was because my sisters and brothers were all married and very prosperous, and I was just working in the post office. He realized that I needed some money. I didn't know anything about hypnosis, and all the accusations were lies."

As she was going through this difficult period, a very wise woman gave Carol a master thought: "Truth shall be my shield and buckler." This is from the 91st Psalm. God is the truth and is the same yesterday, today, and forever. *I am the truth. I am the way. I am the light.* The woman told her that regardless of all the lies, post ponements, expenses, and everything else she was encountering, all she needed to do was to keep affirming her master thought.

It cost Carol $15,000 in legal fees and other expenses, and the case went to an appellate court before it was dismissed. Of course, it cost her relatives a lot of money, too. I told her, "I know you think that you lost that money, but you haven't unless you accept the loss."

I gave her a master thought to focus on: *I am mentally and spiritually identified with that $15,000. It comes back to me magnified and multiplied in Divine order and through Divine love.*

She saw the point. The subconscious always manifests what you give your attention to. If you're involved in a lawsuit like she was, don't let it dominate your thoughts. Focus on a positive master thought instead. Even though her own brothers and sisters were taking false oaths and accusing her unjustly, Carol kept affirming, "The Truth is my shield and buckler."

The nervous, perturbed mind runs off in all directions. A master thought is like a good sheepdog that rounds up all these thoughts that have gone astray, bringing them back to the central place where you want them. For example, if you say, "The Lord is my shepherd. I shall not want," you shall never want for evidence of the fact that the Lord leads you to green pastures and beside still waters—meaning to abundance and peace of mind. This is a wonderful master thought because a shepherd watches over his sheep and loves and cares for them. Tell yourself, "God is like the shepherd who guides and strengthens me," and wonders will unfold in your life.

Some years ago, Owen R. told me that he took a lot of his friends out on a boat. The waves got extremely rough and tossed the boat around, threatening to swamp it. One fellow was terribly agitated and disturbed and was shaking all over. Owen knew, of course, that fear is contagious, so he threw the man a rope and said, "Hold on to that for dear life and you'll be fine. When I say, 'Pull,' pull on the rope, and we'll get to shore safely."

The group did reach land despite the ferocious storm, and the man who'd been so frightened looked at the rope and discovered that it wasn't attached to anything! Owen had given him a master thought that allowed him to get rid of his fear. He focused on this thought until they made their way to shore.

You can also hang on to a master thought when you're worried or upset. You attach to the God Presence within, which is All-Wise and All-Knowing. When the negative thoughts arise or you encounter the propaganda of the world, you remain undisturbed because you have the master thought: *God is my shepherd.*

※✝※

How compulsive are your worries, fears, and anxieties? How fleeting are your thoughts of peace and tranquility? You may say, "I read a psalm, but it means nothing to me—I'm just reading aloud. I'm still full of worry."

Well, you can always overcome something if you think you can. You can do all things through the Divine Power that strengthens you. Nearly everyone knows how impossible it is to fight a domineering, negative thought, but you can. When a harmful emotion such as fear, resentment, or hate comes to you, deal with it immediately. Decapitate it. Don't let evil grow up, become strong, and defeat you, for it will give you sickness and tumors. Replace it with a positive thought and you'll drive it out.

※✝※

A bad habit is a group of negative thoughts repeated frequently until they enter into the subconscious mind and become automatic. Examples of this include worry and poverty. You can change these thought-patterns, however, by deliberately choosing to think about something constructive. You can consciously involve yourself in some activity that will distract you from the problem and put your mind on something constructive.

For instance, suppose that you're involved in a prolonged lawsuit. There are delays and difficulties, and it's becoming extremely expensive and frustrating. As you're driving home from court, instead of thinking about all of the confusion and impediments, say, "The Lord is my light. I dwell in the secret place of the Most High. I abide in the shadow of the Almighty. He is my refuge and my fortress. My God, in Him will I trust."

The God Presence is watching over you, sustaining you, and strengthening you. You're in tune with the Infinite, and you realize that no evil shall befall you. Angels are protecting you. Say, "God's love fills my soul; God's peace floods my mind." You'll overcome all obstacles because the Almighty Presence obliterates all negative patterns and renders harmless all those people who are taking false oaths against you or who are trying to undermine you.

Now what has happened to the fear and worry? You've supplanted them. Make a habit of doing so. Don't fight the negative thoughts—just introduce constructive ones into your mind. Do it again and again, and it will become a good habit. Don't worry about the bad things, for they'll disappear like the sun dissipates the mist. The light of God dissolves the problems in your mind. Yes, God shall come with healing on His wings.

If you say, "I can't stop myself from thinking these dark thoughts. They're troubling me, and I'm at their mercy," that's a big lie, for you can immediately say, "The Lord is my light and salvation. Divine Intelligence is the solution to all of my problems. The Lord is the strength of my life. Of whom shall I be afraid? He shall hide me in His pavilion. In the secret of His tabernacle, He shall protect me."

Undisciplined emotions are like stampeding cattle or wild elephants. They destroy our peace, undermine our health, and ruin our fortune and success in life. When emotions are negative, of course, they have a destructive outlet. On the other hand, constructive emotions heal, bless, and inspire. When your emotions are controlled by Divine love and harmony, the wolf shall lie down with the lamb and not hurt anything. Peace can come to you through the activity of your master thought, which is knowledge of the One Power. It's the *I am* in you—the Life Principle and the Living Spirit Almighty. Affirm, "God's river of peace flows through me."

A man who is suspicious of his wife when she's 15 minutes late and gets angry is looking through the eyes of distrust, which is the dominant idea or master thought in his mind. No marriage can survive such a master thought. If he invited Divine love to govern him instead, it would be wonderful.

Since Spirit is God or the Only Cause, people, circumstances, events, the weather, the stars, the sun, the moon, the apple, and the orange are all effects. You shouldn't make an effect a cause. Don't say, "That fellow is blocking my good," because then you're enthroning other gods in your mind. You're saying, "My spouse is my happiness" or "My father-in-law creates a lot of disturbance in my life and is taking away my peace of mind." In these instances, you're making a person greater than God by saying that he or she is the cause of harmony or distress. This is absurd! The Bible says: "You shall have no other gods before Me."

A woman asked me, "How can I overcome feeling angry and resentful toward my father-in-law, who is living with us now? He's unfriendly and criticizes me, my cooking, housekeeping, and children. I have to live with him."

First of all, the explanation is the cure. I said, "Your father-in-law is in your home, but he isn't God. Are you telling me that he has the power to give you a migraine headache, high blood pressure, or an ulcer? Resentment is the quickest way in the world to get old and wrinkled. If you become bitter, you corrode your soul, and all the face-lifts in the world won't heal it. So stop making him a God. He isn't one and doesn't have any power to disturb you or make you ill.

"Remind yourself that although you temporarily have to live with him, you're living in your own home in Divine order and love. You, your husband, and your children live there; and only God's love can come through the door. Release your father-in-law and let him go. He doesn't belong there."

The woman followed my advice, and her father-in-law left a few days later because she'd released him and refused to give him any more power.

With the Spirit within, your mind is free. You can go wherever you want in your thoughts. You can think the great truths. As you're preparing dinner or vacuuming the floor, you can say: "God is my guide. He watches over me, loves me, and cares for me. He is my shepherd. He leads me to green pastures and still waters. God thinks, speaks, and acts in me. The peace of God reigns supreme in this home."

Where's your mind? It's with God. You're in the secret place where you walk and talk with the Infinite. It's an impregnable fortress, and no one else can enter. It's the only Presence and Power. One with God is a majority, and if God is for you, who can be against you?

The Spiritual Power inspires, heals, strengthens, and restores your mind and body. It's a beneficent and kindly power. It's the spirit within you. It started your heartbeat and grows your nails and the hair on your head. It's God in you, and He knows the answer. Trust Him completely because He responds as mercy, love, inspiration, and beauty.

This Divine Power covers you with Its feathers of love, light, truth, and beauty. Completely reject the negative thoughts of the world, and realize that God's love dissolves the fear patterns of your subconscious mind, which is the terror of the night. Know that you're secure in the invisible hands of the Infinite. You always vibrate with the mind of God, and all is well. You're completely free from fear and worry. You're immunized and God-intoxicated because you received the Divine antibody, the Presence of God in your own heart.

God walks and talks in you, and you live in the joyous expectancy of the best. No evil shall befall you, for God and His holy angels—ideas, impulses, intuition, and guidance—have complete charge over you. You're protected in all of your ways. Your salvation is revealed to you because your greatest prayer is: *How is it in God and heaven?* And the answer flows into your mind: All is bliss, harmony, peace, joy, abundance, and security. When you come to the conclusion in your mind that there's only One Power and that It's guiding you now, your subconscious will respond to that belief.

In a Nutshell

You know that it's impossible for your prayer to fail, so you're not the least bit anxious or tense about whether it will be fulfilled. If you don't get exactly what you ask for, you'll get something grander or greater. Say, "Either this or something greater in your sight, my God, unfolds easily and effortlessly in my life." That's a master thought.

People who fail constantly have a pattern of failure. They have a sense of guilt and feel that they should fail. They're driven by a deep, unconscious impulse. Many have a desire to hurt themselves. They want to inflict punishment on themselves, but they're the only ones condemning themselves.

Everything is in a state of flux. Nothing is forever, and everything passes away. Fortunately, we can control our attitude toward these constant changes. It's not what happens but what we *think* about what happens that's important.

Your master thoughts can bring about wonderful experiences and results because when you change your mind, you change your body. *It is done unto you as you believe.*

Your master thought controls all of your sundry thoughts, moods, propensities, impulses, and tendencies. Therefore, it's wise to focus on the dominant idea that God is your shepherd and supplies all of your needs. As you inject that idea into your subconscious through repetition, it becomes automatic.

A bad habit is a group of negative thoughts repeated frequently until they enter into the subconscious mind and become automatic. Examples of this are worry and poverty. However, you can deliberately choose to think about something constructive. You can consciously involve yourself in some activity that will distract you from the problem. Say, "God is the Source of my supply, and all of my needs are met. God loves and cares for me. He watches over me like a shepherd watches over his sheep." That's a wonderful master thought. If you let it fill your mind, you'll lack for nothing all the days of your life.

Chapter Two

---·•◆•·---

Your Friend, the Subconscious

There are two main spheres of activity within the mind. The conscious mind, which is sometimes called the *objective mind,* is the reasoning component that chooses, analyzes, investigates, scrutinizes, and concludes. For example, you select your books, your home, and your partner in life with this mind.

The subconscious, which is often referred to as the *subjective mind,* is the second sphere, and it accepts whatever is impressed upon it or whatever you consciously believe. It doesn't argue with you about whether your thoughts are good or bad, or true or false—it simply responds according to the nature of your ideas or suggestions. Even if they're erroneous, destructive thoughts work negatively in your subconscious and in due time will come forth into your outer experience as unpleasant results. In addition, the subconscious controls the functioning of your heart and the processes of digestion, circulation, and breathing without any effort on your part.

Your subjective mind performs its highest functions when your objective senses are in abeyance. In other words, the subconscious is the intelligence that manifests when the activity of the conscious mind is suspended or in a sleepy, drowsy state. Your subjective mind sees without using your eyes, and it has the capacity for clairvoyance and clairaudience. It can leave your body, travel to distant lands, and bring back information. Furthermore, using this powerful function, you can read the thoughts of others, view the contents of sealed envelopes, and see inside closed safes.

In order to learn the true art of prayer, it's extremely important that you understand the interaction of your subconscious and conscious mind. When these two aspects function harmoniously, the result is health, peace, joy, and happiness. On the other hand, all of the evil, pain, suffering, war, crime, and sickness in the world is due to the inharmonious relationship of your subconscious and conscious mind.

In the Bible, it says: "The husband is the head of the wife." Unfortunately, theologians have taken this statement literally for thousands of years, and this has held women in bondage. In fact, it's a symbolic statement; the *husband* represents your conscious mind, while the *wife* represents the subconscious. It follows that your subconscious is controlled by your conscious mind. Whatever your conscious mind feels to be true, your subconscious accepts. Your thought is creative, and your capacity to imagine and choose the ideas you entertain gives you power over all creation.

Don't dwell on the imperfections and shortcomings of others because whatever you think and feel about another, you create in your own mind, body, and circumstances. Ask yourself: *Would I like to live with what I'm wishing for someone else?* If the answer is yes, you're on the right track.

The Bible says: "Whatever things you ask when you pray, believe that you receive them, and you will have them." That's a psychological law. Assume the feeling that would be yours as you realize your desire. As you do this, wonderful things will begin to happen in your life.

The subconscious mind always supports life. For example, if someone presents you with a phony deal, its intuitive voice warns you of the danger. If you burn yourself, it seeks to reduce the edema and gives you new skin and tissue. If your son is very sick and you tell your mind that you need to wake up at 2 A.M. to give him medicine, the subconscious will get you up at the needed time even though you're completely exhausted.

Pray, believing that you already possess what you're asking for, and it will come to pass. This is the law of inverse transformation. For example, if you want to sell your house, imagine how you'd feel if you succeeded in your goal. You'd probably feel a certain amount of joy and satisfaction. If you experience that elation in your imagination, your feeling must produce the sale of your home. Imagine the check in your hand, giving thanks for it, depositing it in the bank, and doing all of the things you would do if the sale took place. Awaken within yourself the feeling that would be yours if your desire was realized now.

Steven K. wanted to go to a certain college but got rejected. I said to him, "You understand the law of inverse transformation. How would you feel if they accepted you now? What if you went to see the admissions officer who rejected you and he said, 'Well, we've changed our mind. We've looked over your qualifications again and decided to admit you to our school'?"

Steven answered, "I'd feel happy. I'd call up my dad to share the good news and I'd feel wonderful."

"Well," I said, "as you go to sleep at night, picture me congratulating you on your acceptance and your marvelous success in college. Imagine that you're also talking to your father, telling him that you've been accepted. Go there now in your own mind. The admissions officer is saying, 'We'd like you to come study here.' Wonderful! All right then . . . you can capture that feeling or inner mood in your imagination."

Steven did as I suggested, and he was accepted to his dream college. Yes, if you assume the feeling of an answered prayer and sustain that emotion, it will be fulfilled.

How can you believe you have your desire now? You create a mental picture, dramatize it, and feel its reality. If a physical fact can produce a psychological state, then a psychological state can produce a physical fact. Rejoice in your success! Believe in the law of growth, knowing that the seed you put in the ground will flourish if you nourish, water, and fertilize it.

Your mind is a collection of impressions. Some are good, while perhaps others aren't so wonderful. Your mind should be open only to thoughts that heal, bless, inspire, elevate, and dignify your soul, for ideas are our masters. The reason why there's so much misery in the world is that many people hold beliefs that are negative as well as completely false. These gloomy thoughts get snarled up in the subconscious and must find an outlet. The result is unhappy events and circumstances.

When I use the term *subconscious mind,* I'm not looking at it from a narrow Freudian perspective that focuses on sexual frustrations, inhibitions, and things of that nature. I'm talking about the great universal mind. You can call it the *superconscious, subliminal mind, Allah, Brahma, Reality, Infinite Intelligence, Spirit,* or the *Life Principle*—you can use any name you want.

The important thing to know is that the subconscious is the subjective wisdom and intelligence that controls all of your vital organs when you're sound asleep and sometimes answers your prayer through a dream or a vision. Your subjective mind is active 24 hours a day. It's your greatest friend.

When you say that something is impossible, remember that according to the science of aerodynamics, the bumblebee can't fly because its wingspan is too short and its weight is too great. However, the little insect doesn't know about these laws, so it goes ahead and flies. Therefore, when someone says that something can't be done, use the power of your imagination and say, "It *can* be achieved, and I'm going to do it." Then the subconscious responds and brings it to pass in a wonderful, wonderful way.

Divine Intelligence comes to our aid when we ask It directly for help. There are many cases in which scientists, for example, have prayed for ideas or solutions and received them. Nikola Tesla, a brilliant engineer who brought forth the most amazing innovations, said that when a conception for an invention came into his mind, he would build it in his imagination, knowing that his subconscious would reveal to his conscious mind all the parts needed for its manufacture in concrete form. By quietly contemplating every possible improvement, Tesla didn't have to spend any time correcting defects once his idea was created in the physical world. He said, "Invariably, my device works as I imagined it should. In 20 years, there hasn't been a single exception." His subconscious mind gave him the ideas for all of his inventions.

⚜

A famous chemist, August von Stradonitz, used his subconscious mind to discover the structure of the benzene compound. He'd been working laboriously for years to figure out how the six carbon and six hydrogen atoms of the benzene formula fit together. He was constantly perplexed and unable to solve the matter. Tired and exhausted, he turned the request over to his subconscious mind. Then one night, he had a dream about a snake biting its own tail. This image from his subconscious gave him the long-sought answer of the circular arrangement of the atoms that make up the benzene ring.

Countless inventions and insights come about in this way. In fact, there are numerous references in the Bible to dreams, revelations, and warnings given to people during sleep. For example, the scriptures point out that Joseph earned the praise and recognition of the pharaoh for interpreting the Egyptian ruler's dreams to wisely predict the future. The Bible says: "If there is a prophet among you, I, the Lord [meaning the subconscious mind], make Myself known to him in a vision; I speak to him in a dream."

⚜

In many instances, dreams provide answers to your problems and warn you about investments, journeys, and relationships, as well as the pitfalls of daily living. However, your dreams don't describe an immutable fate. Your subconscious is subject to change, and when you know the Divine laws, you create your own future. You can fill your subconscious with the truths of God, and you'll push everything that is unlike God out of your mind.

I once had a telephone call from a woman in New York City who told me that her husband had confided to her that he planned to take a large sum of money from his safety-deposit box and invest it in a foreign country. A few days later, he passed away. The woman visited the bank and found that the cash was indeed no longer in his box. There was no record of any investment he might have made, and a close inspection of his desk revealed no clues.

I suggested to her that she turn her request over to her subconscious, and it would reveal the answer to her in its own way. She prayed as follows: "My subconscious mind knows where my husband put that money, and I accept the answer and believe implicitly that the solution comes clearly into my conscious mind." She quietly dwelled on the meaning of these words, knowing that they'd be impressed in her subconscious mind, thereby activating its response.

One night shortly thereafter, she had a very vivid dream in which she found a small black box hidden behind a picture of Lincoln on the wall in her husband's den. She was shown in the dream how to press a secret button, which couldn't be seen with the naked eye. When she awakened, she rushed to the den and took down the picture of Lincoln. When she pressed the button revealed in the dream, an opening appeared containing the black box, which held $50,000 in cash.

She'd discovered the treasures of her subconscious and learned that there was a friend within her who knows all and sees all. Like this woman, you can also tap into the wisdom of your subconscious to receive the answers to your prayers.

⊹✦⊹

A young woman in San Francisco experienced the following recurring dream for four consecutive nights: Her fiancé, who was living in Los Angeles, appeared quite suddenly, and an extremely high mountain that seemed impossible to scale rose between them. In her dream, she felt surprised, frustrated, and bewildered; and she awoke with a sense that something was very wrong.

A recurring dream is important because it's the intuitive voice of your subconscious saying to you, "Stop, look, and listen." To better understand the meaning of the dream, I asked the woman what the mountain signified to her, and she said that it symbolized an unsurmountable obstacle.

I then suggested that she speak to her fiancé about the dream to find out if he was hiding anything from her. Accordingly, she flew to Los Angeles to see him. After a heart-to-heart talk, he finally told her, "I'm gay. I wanted to marry you so that my customers, who are very religious, wouldn't suspect anything."

The woman's subconscious prevented her from getting further involved in what ultimately would have been a disastrous marriage. You, too, can exercise the same kind of foresight by analyzing the recurrent themes in your own dreams.

⊹✦⊹

The ancient Hebrews said that we partake in the wisdom and prescience of the gods when we're sound asleep. Furthermore, many dreams are precognitive, allowing us to see events before they happen. We're often given detailed instructions about what action to take. You can use this wonderful power of subconscious intelligence whether you're religious, agnostic, or even atheist.

The Presence of the Infinite is within you, and It works through you even as you sleep. You turn away from the vexations, strife, and contentions of the day; and your conscious mind is in abeyance. Go to sleep in the feeling that you're a tremendous success . . . that you're absolutely outstanding. If you have a problem, contemplate the solution, saying, "Infinite Intelligence gives me the solution, and I accept the answer. It comes to me in Divine order." The subjective self corrects the errors of the day and anchors your thought to the Supreme Intelligence within you.

When successful entrepreneur Arthur R. has a conference and there's an important decision to be made, he closes his eyes, relaxes, and lets go. His associates do the same thing, becoming quiet and still. What do you suppose they think about? They focus on the Infinite Intelligence within them that knows what's best for the organization. They contemplate the harmonious solution in the calm of their own minds. In that relaxed state, the wisdom of the subconscious rises to consciousness. When they open their eyes, they know the best decision to make.

When your motivation is right, your choices will be sound. If your motivation is wrong, no matter what you do, your actions will be misguided. Therefore, when you need to make a decision, ask yourself: *What's my motivation?* Then say, "Infinite Intelligence guides me and reveals the answer to me." If your intentions are good, whatever you do will be right.

Robert C., who lives in Albuquerque, New Mexico, knows a number of Indian medicine men there. He told me an interesting story about an Indian woman who was very ill. A special medicine man came in to help, and the members of their tribe set out a pot of boiling water. The proof of a true medicine man is that he can put his arm into boiling water for about ten minutes without experiencing a burn or inflammation of any kind. That's a sure sign that he's disciplined and has served his apprenticeship.

After the medicine man had been tested, he put some blankets on the sick woman and chanted some prayers and holy songs based upon their tribal beliefs. Then he lay down beside the woman and went to sleep, calling upon the Great Spirit.

When he awoke, he said, "The Great Spirit has healed her." Now, what did he mean by that? Well, he came believing in a healing, and in this quiet state of mind, he'd chanted. The woman, of course, was open-minded and ready to receive. She had full faith and confidence in the intelligence and healing power within the medicine man, and she completely recovered. That's what we call *prayer therapy* or *spiritual treatment.* It's simply dwelling upon the Infinite Spirit and Power within you. *According to your faith, it is done unto you.*

There's only one Healing Presence, you see. When you pray for someone as the medicine man did, don't dwell on symptoms, fever, or anything like that. Just focus upon the intelligence, wisdom, vitality, wholeness, beauty, and perfection of the Infinite, knowing that It sustains and strengthens the person you're treating for. Then the Presence of God will be resurrected in him or her. That's the basis of all healing.

Dr. Elsie McCoy is a clear example of what using the law of mind can accomplish. Ever since she was 18 years old, she has made it a habit to affirm: "Only Divine right action takes place in my life, and whatever I need to know is revealed to me instantly by the Infinite Intelligence within me."

As a young woman, she was engaged to a prominent surgeon in Chicago. They were separated by over a thousand miles due to their different assignments. One night while she was sound asleep, she had a vivid dream that her fiancé was dating a nurse. He was saying to the other woman, "You know I'm engaged, but she's a thousand miles away and knows nothing about us."

Elsie phoned him the next day and told him about the "silly dream" she'd had and laughed about it. However, he was furious and accused her of having employed detectives to spy on him. With that, she dissolved the engagement. The wisdom of her subconscious had protected her from what would undoubtedly have been a tragic marriage.

The subjective mind can also protect you if only you'll listen to it. Some people brush these things aside and say, "It was only a dream." However, there's such a thing as precognition—seeing events before they happen. If you foresee something negative happening to yourself or someone else, you can take steps to avoid misfortune.

Louise Wright, a member of my staff, was informed many years ago by a surgeon that she needed an operation on her left foot that would require putting her leg in a cast as well as using crutches for two months or longer. She prayed that the Infinite Intelligence would direct her to the right decision. She turned this request over to her subconscious mind every evening, and after four days, she had a dream about a doctor who was a family friend telling her that surgery wasn't necessary.

The next day, she went to visit him, and he told her that he could give her some adjustments and she could do some exercises to bring perfect alignment back to her foot. In fact, a perfect healing followed. Through her dream, her subconscious had revealed to her exactly what she needed to know.

⊹✛⊹

About ten years ago, Dr. Arthur Thomas started attending my Sunday lectures. He told me, "I suddenly realized that my thought was the only creative power and that I was going to create what I really wanted." Consequently, he began to affirm to himself frequently: "I am a minister now; I am teaching the truths of life to people." Every night he would imagine that he was expounding on the great truths to a wonderful group of men and women in a church.

He continued to think along these lines for a month or so, then decided to take the ministerial course at the church of Religious Science here in Los Angeles. He was confident of the end result because he'd already imagined and felt as true the reality of that which he envisioned in his mind. He passed all the tests and examinations in Divine order and was offered a position as minister at a church in Pasadena immediately after finishing his classes.

He's now doing exactly what he decreed mentally. He knew that his subconscious mind would respond to thoughts. That's the meaning of the biblical passage: "It shall be done to you according to your faith."

⊹✛⊹

During a trip to Mexico two years ago, I met a minister who had a pronounced facial tic in his right eye that was very humiliating for him. He'd received injections to paralyze the nerve, but after some months, the problem flared up again. The condition became particularly acute when he spoke before his congregation or at other social gatherings. He'd reached the point where he was actually contemplating resigning because of people's comments and his own sense of embarrassment. He said, "A lot of people are distracted from my sermons because of my tic, and some women think I'm flirting with them."

During our prolonged discussion, I told him that I had a deep inner feeling that he had a profound sense of hurt and probably a guilt complex that he was unwilling to face. The tic affecting his eye might symbolize something that he didn't want to look at in his life.

He admitted freely that he no longer believed in what he was teaching, which made him feel guilty. However, he was afraid to resign because he felt that he couldn't make a living outside of the ministry. He deeply resented the members of his church board, who criticized him whenever he deviated from the orthodox standards of teaching. All of this pressure and his failure to admit to his congregation that he no longer believed the dogma of the church was converted by his subconscious mind into a nervous tic.

I suggested to him that on following Sunday when he was back from his vacation, he should speak freely from his pulpit and tell his church members that he was resigning since he no longer believed in what he was preaching. He understood that to teach one thing and believe another created a powerful negative conflict in the mind, resulting in mental and physical disorders.

In a letter to me, he described what happened next: "I felt a tremendous relief and a great sense of peace came over me. My constant affirmation was: 'Thou will show me the path of life.' And one of my former board members gave me a position as personnel director in his organization, where I'm now happy."

If you have a problem—whether it's mental, physical, or emotional—ask yourself: *What am I turning away from? What is it I don't want to look at? Am I hiding my resentment and hostility for someone?* Face the problem. Solve it with the knowledge of your deeper mind, knowing that the Life Principle always seeks to heal and restore. Infinite Spirit never condemns or punishes—It can't. All judgment is given to "the son," which is your own mind. You fashion your own destiny, for as you think in your heart or sub-conscious, so are you.

Realize, therefore, that thoughts are things, you attract what you feel, and you become what you imagine. Amazing events will begin unfold in your life if you do so, because there's only One Power—and this Power is within *you*. You're the captain on the bridge giving the orders; your subconscious mind will accept the thoughts you feed it and bring them to pass, whether they're posi-tive or negative.

⚜

A few years ago, I had a most interesting conversation with an old friend, whom I had known previously in India—I'll call him "Harry." He's a medical doctor who has tremendous faith in spiri-tual healing and has used clairvoyance and astral projection for many years.

While he was visiting India, his daughter—who was studying in Honolulu—had become extremely ill and was at the point of death. A cable about her condition was sent to him in Calcutta. When he received it, he adopted a yoga posture, closed his eyes, and got into a quiet, receptive state of mind. He visualized his fourth-dimensional or astral body emerging through his head, and he decreed with deep conviction: "I want to appear instantly to my daughter and minister to her."

He repeated this command about six times then dropped off into a profound slumber. Immediately he found himself at his daughter's bedside. She was asleep but woke up instantly and exclaimed to him, "Dad, why didn't you tell me you were coming? Help me!" He placed his hands upon her and chanted certain religious phrases. He told her, "You will arise in a few hours and be well."

She had a wonderful healing. Her fever immediately subsided, and she shouted to the nurse, "I'm healed! I'm well! My father was here, and he cured me." The nurse thought that her patient was delirious, but the resident physician that she was indeed perfectly healthy. However, they both laughed at her story about being visited by her dad from India. The nurse was perplexed and asked, "How could your father or anybody else get in from downstairs through closed doors? I saw no one enter your room."

The daughter explained, "My father visited me in his fourth-dimensional body. He laid his hands on me and prayed with me." But the nurse said, "I don't believe in ghosts, apparitions, or voodoo." Then the young woman realized that further explanations would be useless.

Harry told me that he remained completely conscious throughout his experience and had left his physical body for just ten minutes in all. He realized that his presence gave his daughter a tremendous transfusion of faith, confidence, and courage that filled her subconscious mind. According to her belief, it was done unto her. These are the wonderful powers of the friend within you . . . the deeper mind.

In a Nutshell

Your subconscious accepts what you impress upon it and reproduces it in your life. Select only what is true, lovely, noble, and godlike.

Pray, believing that you already possess your desire, and it will come to pass. Go to sleep in the feeling that you're a tremendous success and are absolutely outstanding. If you have a problem, contemplate the solution, saying, "Infinite Intelligence gives me the solution, and I accept the answer. It comes to me in Divine order." Your subjective mind corrects the errors of the day and anchors your thought to the Supreme Intelligence within you.

If you have a problem—whether it's mental, physical, or emotional—ask yourself: *What am I turning away from? What is it I don't want to look at? Am I hiding my resentment and hostility for someone?* Face the problem and solve it with the knowledge of your deeper mind, knowing that the Life Principle always seeks to heal and restore. You're the captain giving the orders, and your subconscious will accept all of the thoughts you feed it and bring them to fruition in your life.

Chapter Three

The Unbelievable Power
of Suggestion

*I*f you believe people who call you *stupid, dumb,* or *ignorant,*
your subconscious mind will respond accordingly. However,
other people's thoughts have no power unless you believe them.
When your thoughts are God's thoughts, Divine power is with
your thoughts of good. Since God is for you, who on earth can be
against you?

⚜

A few years ago, I complimented a young saleswoman in a
department store. I said, "You're very beautiful and charming."
She protested, "Oh no, I'm not!" I asked her, "What makes you
think that?" She answered, "My mother told me that I'm awkward,
ungainly, and very plain."

The woman truly believed her mom's criticism and was full
of bitterness, resentment, and conflict. I told her that her mother
had probably said such harsh things to her out of jealousy, for her
daughter was clearly lovely, engaging, and articulate. I also advised
her to practice the following affirmation: "I am a child of God and

a daughter of the Infinite. I am illumined and inspired. I am happy, joyous, and free."

As she continued to pray in this way, she was transformed and is no longer down on herself. She exalts God in the midst of her, for He is the Living Spirit Almighty Who created everyone and everything.

Judge Troward, a leader in the New Thought movement, wrote: "Once you admit there is any power outside yourself, however beneficent you may conceive it to be, you have sown the seed which must sooner or later bear the fruit of fear, which is the entire ruin of life, love, and liberty."

You should write this truth indelibly on your heart and think about it a thousand times a day.

Dr. Paul Tournier, a well-known physician in Europe, said that doctors should stop making negative suggestions because people look upon them as authorities. If a physician says, "You're going to be deaf in a year's time," you may indeed lose your hearing within 12 months. Similarly, if a trusted doctor tells you that you're going to lose your vision, you may proceed to go blind unless you counteract this destructive suggestion.

Dr. Brant, a New Thought minister in South Africa, told me about the widespread belief in voodoo in his country. So when I visited a particular mine there where about 9,000 men were employed, I spoke to the local doctor about the belief in curses. He said, "It's true. If one of these workers is given a skull and crossbones and told that he's been cursed and will die at 6 o'clock, at precisely that time, the man will sit down and die." The doctor continued, "In fact, these men kill *themselves* through their own fear and mistaken beliefs. They've been brought up to believe in the power of voodoo, and their subconscious beliefs always manifest in the exterior world."

Realize that all power lies in the movement of your *own* thought. No one has the ability to hurt you but yourself. You can use the following prayer: "I will fear no evil for thou art with me. Thy rod and thy staff, they comfort me. I dwell in the secret place of the Most High. I abide in the shadow of the Almighty. He is my refuge and my fortress. My God, in Him will I trust."

Identify yourself with these great, eternal truths and you'll build up Divine immunity. You'll become God-intoxicated and will walk the earth with the praise of the Almighty forever on your lips.

Dr. Bayles was a great New Thought teacher in Los Angeles who'd studied medicine in London. He told a group of us that during his training, he and the other interns would sometimes give patients a placebo—just a little sugar or milk in capsule form—and tell them, "This is a new drug that will cure your problem and take away your pain."

The patients would come back the next week and say, "Oh doctor, that was marvelous medicine. I need some more."

This story reveals the power of suggestion. Dr. Bayles released the healing power of the patients, and they accepted it. In the same way, a doctor can hypnotize you and remove a tumor, growth, or even a leg; and you'll feel absolutely nothing. Why? Because as you're hypnotized, the physician makes a suggestion that you'll feel no pain, and lo and behold, you don't!

Dr. Elsie McCoy, who was a chief surgical nurse in a Chicago hospital for many years, describes postoperative patients who were in such pain that they cried out in the night and asked for morphine. She told me, "I'd often put half a cc of distilled water in a syringe and say, 'All right, my dear. I'm going to give you half a grain of morphine subcutaneously.' Then I'd give them the injection of water, and they'd go off to sleep for 12 hours. All of their pain was taken away."

What happened? The patients accepted her suggestion and believed that a powerful drug would make them feel better—and according to their belief, it was done unto them. This is the marvelous power of the mind.

Dr. David Seabury taught me Phineas Parkhurst Quimby's techniques of healing many years ago. He also told me an interesting story about an experiment he and his friends had conducted on a young man, a ne'er-do-well who lived in their little town in Northern California.

Every day this man would go to the post office, the coffee shop, and the bar. Dr. Seabury and his friends decided to have some fun with him and got the postal clerk, waitress, and bartender to participate in the prank. When the man went to the post office, the clerk said, "You don't look good. There's yellow pigmentation around your eyes, and your face is flushed. Have you seen a doctor? Are you all right? Shouldn't you be in bed?"

Then the man went into the coffee shop, and the waitress asked him, "Have you been to the doctor? You don't look well. How's your blood pressure?"

Then when he went to the bar, the bartender said, "Your eyes seem yellowish, and you look faint. Shouldn't you see a doctor?"

Dr. Seabury said, "The man went home and became deathly ill. He called me, and I had to go tell him that it was all a joke and that he'd made himself sick by accepting negative suggestions."

Remember that your subconscious accepts the thoughts that are impressed upon it and brings them to pass as conditions, experiences, and events. It doesn't argue with you or reason things out like your conscious mind does. It's therefore vital that you choose thoughts and ideas that bless, heal, inspire, and fill your soul with joy.

Innumerable experiments by psychologists, psychiatrists, and others on people in a hypnotic state have shown that the subconscious mind will accept any suggestion, however false it may be. For example, if a skilled hypnotist suggests that you are Napoléon Bonaparte, or even a cat or a dog, you'll act out the part with complete accuracy. If you're instructed to kneel down, you will. If you're ordered to bark or lap up milk like a dog, you will.

The suggestion implanted in your mind continues to operate even after the hypnosis is over. For instance, if you're told under hypnosis that at 3 o'clock the next day you'll jump up three times and sing "Twinkle, Twinkle, Little Star," sure enough, the following afternoon at the proscribed time, you'll suddenly leap up from your desk three times and sing that song.

You must realize that your conscious mind is the sentry at the gate. Its chief function is to protect your subconscious from false or destructive beliefs.

People react in different ways to the same suggestion because of their subconscious conditioning or belief. For instance, suppose you approach a passenger aboard a ship and say something like, "You look ill. You're very pale, and I feel certain that you're going to be seasick. Let me help you to your cabin." Your suggestion plays into her own indwelling fears and belief in the possibility of becoming seasick, and she begins to feel nauseated. On the other hand, if you go up to a sailor on the ship and say to him sympathetically, "My dear fellow, are you feeling all right? You look to me as if you were going to be seasick," you'll get a different response. According to his temperament, he'll either laugh at you or express a mild irritation. Your suggestion falls on deaf ears in this case because he has no subconscious belief that he is prone to seasickness. He has already convinced himself of his immunity.

You must remember that a suggestion can't be imposed on the subconscious against the will of the conscious mind. You have the power to reject any negative thought or idea. For example, the passenger could say, "I'm going to roll with the blows and have the time of my life. I'm going to have the most wonderful experience on this trip." She would thereby neutralize your negative suggestion.

Every two or three years, I give a series of lectures at the Truth Forum in London. Dr. Evelyn Fleet, a distinguished psychologist, is the director of that forum. She told me about an article that had appeared in the English newspapers about a man whose daughter had a crippling form of arthritis and an "incurable" skin disease. Medical treatment had failed to alleviate her condition, and the father had an intense longing for his daughter to be healed. For two years, he kept saying, "I'd give my right arm to see my daughter cured."

As the newspapers described, one day the family got into a serious car accident. The dad's right arm was torn off at the shoulder, and immediately the daughter's arthritis and skin condition vanished. That's a terrible price to pay for a healing, isn't it? The subconscious can't take a joke because it takes everything literally. You'd be wise to stop giving it destructive suggestions and only feed it ideas that heal, bless, elevate, and inspire you in all your ways. It takes you at your word, so stop saying, "I can't be healed" or "I can't make ends meet." Your subconscious will see to it that your thought manifests.

❈

A young singer was invited to give an audition. She'd been looking forward to it, but on three previous occasions, she'd performed miserably because of her fear of failure. She had a good voice but had been saying to herself, "When the time comes for me to sing, maybe they won't like me. I'll try, but I'm scared and am likely to mess up." Her subconscious mind accepted these negative suggestions and proceeded to bring them into her experience.

She overcame her thought-pattern by using the following technique: Three times a day, she isolated herself in her room. She sat down comfortably in an armchair, relaxed her body, and closed her eyes. She imagined that she was as relaxed as a wet leaf on a log. Physical inertia favors mental placidity and renders the mind more receptive to ideas and suggestions. She counteracted her thoughts of fear by saying to herself, "God is the great singer and musician within me. He is the Living Spirit Almighty. I sing beautifully, majestically, and gloriously. I am poised, serene, and confident."

She repeated this statement slowly, quietly, and with feeling for five to ten minutes at each sitting, knowing that whatever we attach to the *I am,* we become. At the end of a week, she was completely calm and confident, and she gave a wonderful audition.

❈

A 75-year-old woman was in the habit of saying to herself, "I'm losing my memory." In fact, you can't actually lose your mind or your memory. Everything that you've ever learned—even in your mother's womb—is recorded faithfully in your subconscious. This deeper mind is the storehouse of memory and forgets nothing.

She reversed her belief and affirmed, "My memory is improving in every way. I always remember whatever I need to know. My impressions are clear and definite, and I retain them automatically and with ease. Whatever I wish to recall immediately presents itself in the correct form in my mind. I am improving rapidly every day, and my memory is now better than it has ever been before."

At the end of three weeks, her memory was back to normal, and she was delighted. She'd impressed new thoughts on her subconscious mind, and they manifested themselves in her experience.

Whatever *you* impress on your subconscious mind will also be expressed on the screen of space. Yes, it will come forth as form, function, experience, and event.

⊨✛⊨

The dictators, despots, and tyrants of the world have used the principles of the subconscious to control people who don't understand the laws of mind. They've appealed to the biases and prejudices of the citizens and fanned their emotions—and if you're emotionally aroused, you can be manipulated. Stalin, Hitler, and Osama bin Laden planted suggestions in the minds of their followers and repeated certain ideas over and over again until the poison manifested in the external world in the form of war, genocide, and misery. It's obviously extremely dangerous to get carried away by negative emotions and blindly accept the hypnotic suggestions of others.

⊨✛⊨

From infancy on, most of us have been given many negative suggestions. Not knowing how to thwart them, we unconsciously accepted them. If you reflect for a moment, you can easily recall how your parents, friends, teachers, and ministers may have contributed to a campaign of negative suggestions. Here are some of the destructive things you might have been told: "You can't," "You'll never amount to anything," "You shouldn't," "You'll fail," "You don't have a chance," "You're all wrong," "It's no use," "It's not what you know but *who* you know," "The world is going to the dogs," "Nobody cares," "Things are getting worse and worse," "Life is an endless grind," "Love is for the birds," "You just can't win," "You can't trust a soul" . . . and so on.

These are all commands to your subconscious mind. Study the things you were taught and you'll discover that the purpose of much of it was to control how you think, feel, and act—or to instill fear into you. This process goes on in every home, office, factory, and club.

If you continue to accept the destructive impressions made on your subconscious in the past, your life will be a living hell. You'll be frustrated, neurotic, and inhibited. However, you can choose to reject them and fill your mind with a constructive pattern of prayer. For example, you can read the Psalms before you go to sleep to counteract negative ideas.

⇥✚⇤

Some years ago, a relative of mine went to a fortune-teller who told him that he had a bad heart and predicted that he would die at the next new moon. He told his family about this prediction and arranged his will. The powerful suggestion of the "psychic" entered into his subconscious mind because he accepted it completely. He died as predicted, not knowing that he was the cause of his own death. An autopsy showed that there was nothing at all wrong with his heart. He'd killed himself through his own thought. I suppose that many of us have heard similar ridiculous stories.

Let's look at what happened in the light of our knowledge of the way the subconscious works. Whatever the conscious, reasoning mind believes, the subconscious mind will accept and act upon. My relative was happy, healthy, and robust when he went to see the fortune-teller. She gave him an extremely negative suggestion, which he accepted. He became terrified and constantly dwelled upon the fact that he was going to die soon. He proceeded to tell everyone about it and prepared for his demise. He brought about the destruction of his physical body through his fear and expectation.

The woman who predicted his death had no more power than the stones and sticks in the field. Her suggestion had no real power, and if he'd known the laws of mind, he would have completely rejected her prediction and said, "My life is God's life; I live forever." He would have refused to give her words any credence, knowing in his heart that he was governed and controlled by his own thoughts and feelings. Like tin arrows aimed at a battleship, her destructive suggestion could have been completely neutralized and dissipated without hurting him.

Remember that other people's suggestions have absolutely no power over you unless you give them power. You have to give your mental consent to an idea for it to have any influence over you. You have the capacity to choose, and you can pick those things that are lovely and good.

⊨✛⊨

Long before ether was discovered, Dr. James L. Dale performed more than 400 major operations without using anesthetic. Instead, he employed the power of hypnosis during surgeries that included amputations, the removal of tumors, and procedures on the eyes, ears, and throat. He also taught his medical assistants to hypnotize patients and tell them after the operation, "You have no infection. Your wound heals quickly, and you feel wonderful." Infection was reduced to a minimum, and Dr. Dale had a mortality rate of only

2 to 3 percent. Isn't that a wonderful example of what you can accomplish with constructive suggestions?

Recently I received a letter from a waiter in Honolulu whom I had met on a recent trip there. He wrote that someone was practicing black magic against him and that everything was going wrong in his life. He mentioned the name of the man whom he believed was using voodoo against him. Remember that *curses, sorcery,* and *Satan* are just words used to disguise people's gross ignorance. There is only *One* Power, and when you use that Power negatively, you can call it *witchcraft, voodoo,* or anything under the sun. But that's all it is. It's a power, but it's not *the* Power—the *I am* and the God Presence within. It's omnipotent and supreme, and nothing can oppose or thwart it. That's why one with God is a majority.

I wrote the waiter a lengthy response, pointing out that all the water in the ocean can't sink a ship unless it gets inside. Likewise, someone else's negative thoughts can't enter his mind unless he opens the door and lets them in.

I stated that it's an indisputable truth that God is all there is. God is absolute truth, boundless love, infinite life, and eternal joy. I told him that his thought is creative and that the Divine Power forever backs his ideas of good. When he thinks of God's love, peace, and joy, he's automatically protected and immune to all of the toxic effluvia of the mass mind. Furthermore, when he dwells on the eternal verities, it's God thinking through him. Whatever God thinks can only result in Divine law and order.

I gave him the following spiritual prescription that you can also use: Sit down quietly two or three times a day and imagine that you're surrounded by a sacred circle of God's light. As you continue to do this, you'll actually see a golden sphere of healing light all around you. This is an emanation of the God Presence within you and renders you impervious to all harm. You're now invulnerable and completely insulated from the fear thoughts or negative suggestions of others. Make a habit of doing this process whenever you think of the voodoo man. Simply affirm: "God's love fills my soul, and I release him. God's love fills his soul, too."

I explained, "You see, if you can't give something, you can't receive it. If you can't hate a person, you can't receive hate; and if you can't wish failure upon someone, you can't receive failure either. Conversely, you also can't receive anything that you can't give. Therefore, be glad to give out love, goodwill, peace, and harmony. Wish for everyone all of the blessings of heaven. It's so simple that a child can understand it."

The sequel to this was most interesting. The waiter used this prayer process, and at the end of a week, he read in the newspaper that the voodoo man had dropped dead in the street—presumably of a heart attack. The explanation for his death is very simple: The waiter stopped receiving the man's negative thoughts and instead poured out benedictions and prayers. As a result, the man's curses had nowhere to go, and the proverbial boomerang took place. His negative emotions recoiled with double force back upon himself, and he actually caused his own death.

If you're wishing death for another, you're thinking about it and feeling it and will create it in your *own* mind and body. Perhaps the other person is full of love and goodwill and therefore can't receive your hostile thoughts. Then who bears their brunt? You do—and they come back to you with double force.

⊰✚⊱

Remember that you're the only thinker in your universe. Since your thought is creative, what you're thinking about the other, you're creating within yourself. That's why the golden rule is the great law.

⊰✚⊱

There were two doctors who were identical twins. One was a student of the Science of Mind and was deeply involved in prayer, meditation, and mystic visioning. The other took up numerology and astrology, not knowing that these things have no actual power unless you believe in them. He was told that according to his astrological chart, he could expect a lot of loss and tragedy. Well, during the course of his life, the man who believed in the stars had a terrible accident, lost his house in a fire, and was sued. In addition, he was disciplined by the medical authorities, and one of his children had a drug overdose and killed himself.

In contrast, the other brother prospered, was honored in foreign countries, and had a most wonderful life. Yes, one brother believed in prayer, while the other believed in astrology. Their story shows us that we must not believe in the stars but in the God Who created them.

I was visited by a young woman who was emotionally distraught because a palmist had predicted that she would have a serious accident on or near her 21st birthday. She'd accepted the suggestion and was consequently afraid to travel or go anywhere. She was living in perpetual fear and impressed her subconscious mind with the belief in an accident. It would undoubtedly have come to pass had she not learned how to neutralize her negative thought.

She affirmed: "Whenever I go somewhere by bus, foot, automobile, train, plane, or any other means of conveyance, I know that Divine love goes before me, making my path joyous, glorious, and safe. I know that Infinite Intelligence guides and directs me at all times and that I am always in the sacred center of God's eternal love. God protects me at all times. He controls all travel in the heavens above and the earth beneath."

She repeated these truths morning, afternoon, and night, knowing that their spiritual vibrations would obliterate the negative suggestion of the palmist from her subconscious mind. In fact, she experienced the happiest day of her life on her 21st birthday when she got married to a childhood friend. She's now 23 years old, and they're extremely happy.

It isn't the stars, a crystal ball, or your genes that mold your destiny—it's your thought-patterns. You mold and fashion your future by using your own mind. *All things whatsoever ye shall ask in prayer, believing, ye shall receive.*

⊰✦⊱

Insist on harmony, health, peace, and abundance. If you say, "It's hopeless, and there's no cure. I must put up with this arthritis (or this lumbago or whatever it is)," then you're doomed. All the prayers in the world won't help you because you're resigned to poor health. In fact, God's will for you is a greater measure of life, love, truth, and beauty transcending your fondest dreams. You must insist on a healing. Don't get angry at yourself or become impatient because then you'll only get worse. Say, "There *is* a solution; and I experience peace, love, and wholeness in my life."

Yes, realize that your own thoughts and feelings create your destiny. Begin now to believe, claim, and feel that God is guiding you in all your ways. Divine right action governs you at all times, and you're inspired from on high. As you accept these truths with your conscious mind, your subconscious will bring all these things to pass, and you'll discover that your path is peaceful and pleasant.

In a Nutshell

Realize that all power lies in the movement of your own thought. No one has the power to hurt you but yourself. Since God is for you, who can be against you?

You have the power to reject any negative thoughts and give your subconscious mind the pattern of prayer by doing things such as reading the Psalms before you go to sleep.

The suggestions of others have absolutely no power whatsoever over you except the power that you give them through your own thought. You have to give your mental consent to ideas before they can influence you. Remember that you have the capacity to choose whatever is lovely and good.

Sit down quietly two or three times a day and imagine that a sacred circle of God's light surrounds you. As you continue to do this, you'll actually see a golden halo of healing light all around you. This is an emanation of the God Presence within that renders you impervious to all harm. You're now invulnerable and completely insulated from the fear thoughts or negative suggestions of others. Simply affirm: "God's love fills my soul."

Whatever you decide to be true in your conscious mind, you'll experience through your subconscious. Therefore, believe that God or Infinite Intelligence is guiding you. Right action reigns supreme, and Divine law and order govern you.

⌖ ⌖

Chapter Four

Practical Meditation

*M*editation isn't mysterious. In fact, everybody meditates. But this doesn't necessarily mean that everyone does so constructively, harmoniously, or peacefully. For example, if you find yourself lost in memories of old hurts, peeves, or grudges of any kind, you're engaged in a full-blown meditation. However, it's an extremely negative one and will have destructive results because whatever you give your attention to, your subconscious magnifies and multiplies. Similarly, if you're thinking about the losses you suffered in the stock market, the tire blowout on the lonely road, or how you were dumped by your high-school sweetheart, you're also dwelling on thoughts that will produce a harmful outcome.

Forget about the past and reach for the wonderful things that are before you, including health, happiness, peace, and vitality. Turn enthusiastically to what is noble and godlike.

When you find yourself listening to news reports filled with predictions of gloom and doom, hunger, and war, you're meditating because you're in a passive, receptive state. Do you want to be hypnotized by all sorts of negative suggestions? No! You have to reject them and say, "I don't accept that." Instead, read a psalm or an inspirational poem before you go to sleep at night. You'll charge your subconscious mind with spiritual truths as you slumber.

If you discover as you drive along the road that you're quarreling mentally with your boss or somebody in the office and are feeling angry, you're indulging in a meditation with very poor results. You see, *meditation* means the conversation you have inside yourself. It's what you say to yourself when you're all alone. That inner speech always manifests in your life because that's what you really believe.

If you pour clean water into a dirty vessel, what happens? The water becomes murky. The vessel symbolizes your mind, which you need to keep pure. If you're full of hostile thoughts, you certainly can't meditate or contemplate the eternal verities. Therefore, when you pray or meditate, forgive yourself for harboring any kind of negative thoughts and forgive everybody on the face of the earth. Surrender them to the God Presence and pray for them to enjoy health, happiness, and all of the blessings of life. You must do this until you can peacefully meet these individuals in your mind and rejoice at hearing good news about them.

Meditation is really the practice of the Presence of God. Whenever your attention wanders away in fear, doubt, or resentment, bring it back to the contemplation of Infinite Spirit. See God everywhere—in all people, trees, sermons, running brooks, and stones.

Don't say that you can't meditate. Of course you can! Don't say, "I have to take lessons in meditation. I'm not spiritual enough and need some special training." All of that is nonsense because you and everybody else are *always* meditating. For example, if you get up in the morning and see that a stock you own has gone down, you may become angry because you've lost money. You're mad at the broker, yourself, and the organization you invested in. You want to write a letter to the company's board of directors to tell them that they're not running their business properly. You fuss and fume and get highly agitated. You've engaged in a deep contemplation, but it's a highly negative one.

Other people may meditate on horse races. They go to the track, lose a lot of money, and begin to dwell upon why they didn't pick the winning horse. They mope about how much they've gambled away, are mad at the jockey, and so on. That's also a meditation with extremely destructive results.

Instead of obsessing about the stock market or races, you can meditate on the fact that God is guiding you now and Divine love fills your soul, making your path perfect and straight. You can focus on something wonderful like this verse from Psalm 1: "But his delight is in the law of the Lord, and in His law he meditates day and night. He will be like a tree firmly planted by streams of water, which yields its fruit in its season . . . and in whatever he does, he prospers."

Psalms are the songs of God and a magnificent tool for meditation.

To meditate is to absorb the great truths and incorporate them in your soul. Just as an apple you eat becomes part of your bloodstream, the truths of God must become a living part of you. When they do, you'll be compelled to express them in your life, and you'll be kind, noble, godlike, and gracious. Follow the injunction of the psalmist who wrote: "Let the words of my mouth and the meditation of my heart be acceptable in Your sight, O Lord, my rock and my Redeemer."

Meditation is the fastest way to become illumined, inspired, and absorbed in the moment that lasts forever. You become engrossed in the Divine Presence within, intensely affirming that the Living Spirit is the only Power, Cause, and Substance. Everything that you're aware of is part of the Infinite Being. Sit quietly and focus your attention on this greatest of all truths. Then you're truly meditating.

Many people meditate on old hurts, grievances, and mistakes they've made. They don't realize that they're magnifying their trouble. For example, if you're dwelling on what the prophets of doom are predicting, or if you're mentally arguing with your boss, you're indulging in a contemplation that will lead to unpleasant results because your silent conversation with yourself always manifests in your experience. Therefore, if a negative thought comes into your mind, neutralize it with a prayer such as: "God is love, and His peace fills my soul."

Dwell on the Infinite Presence and Power and remind yourself that God is boundless love and absolute harmony. He is the Only Cause and Substance. Contemplating what this truth means to you is the highest form of meditation.

Think quietly about the Divine Presence and give your loyalty and devotion to God Who created you and everything in the entire world. Then you'll begin to see peace instead of discord, love instead of hatred, and joy instead of sadness. The results of your meditation will shine forth as peace, joy, gentleness, goodness, faith, temperance, health, vitality, and abundance.

You're Spirit and always will be. A billion years from now, you'll be alive somewhere because you're the Living Spirit Almighty walking the earth. We're all garments that God wears as He moves through the illusion of time and space. God is life, and He is being you now.

I once met a man in a prison in New York City who admitted that he'd killed someone. He had an intense desire, however, to transform himself both mentally and spiritually. He wanted to do great things and contribute to humanity. I advised him to become quiet for 15 to 20 minutes several times every day and contemplate the qualities and attributes of God. He was to silently and lovingly claim and feel that God's love, peace, beauty, glory, and light were flowing through his mind and heart, purifying and restoring his soul.

As he did this regularly, he activated and resurrected the qualities of the Infinite resident in his subjective depths. After about a month, as he meditated one night, this man's entire mind and body—as well as the prison cell he was in—became a blaze of light. He was actually blinded by its intensity for a while. He told me that he felt the ecstasy and rapture of Divine love permeating every atom of his being. The feeling was indescribable, he said. He experienced the moment that lasts forever and was transformed. He began to teach others how to live and was compelled by his subconscious to bring forth and express the fruits of the Spirit, which are love, joy, peace, gentleness, faith, and temperance.

When you contemplate the meaning of the psalms, you're meditating. For example, you can focus on the verse from Psalm 23: "The Lord is my shepherd; I shall not want." A shepherd watches over his sheep and loves them. At night, he checks them to remove thorns or anything that might hurt them. He leads them to the shade when it's hot outside and makes sure that there are no noxious weeds in the fields where they graze. In short, he protects the sheep in every way.

When you choose God or Infinite Intelligence as your shepherd, you'll never want for evidence of the fact that you've chosen the One Power as your guide and source. The psalm tells you exactly what happens when you choose God: "He maketh me to lie down in green pastures; He leadeth me beside the still waters. He restoreth my soul. " In other words, the Infinite Almighty leads you to joy, peace, and fulfillment. Yes, you'll lie down in green pastures as God prospers you spiritually, financially, and intellectually beyond your wildest dreams. You'll find yourself beside still waters as you claim that the river of peace floods your mind, heart, and entire being.

You can sit under a tree, close your eyes, and meditate on the following words: "Divine Intelligence guides me in all my ways. I shall never lack for anything because God guides me. He is a lamp unto my feet and a light upon my path. My mind is now serene. It reflects God's heavenly truths and light. My soul is restored, for God's love dissolves everything unlike itself. His peace floods my mind and heart. I think of the Holy Presence within me all day long. I walk the path of righteousness. I know that there is no death, and I fear no evil, for God is with me. I know that God did not give me a fearful spirit, but a loving and powerful one. God's love and truth comfort, sustain, and nourish me."

Of course, you know that all of your "enemies" are in your own mind. They are: doubt, fear, anger, resentment, and self-condemnation. These are the antagonists that you generate by yourself, and they'll cease to exist if you don't indulge in negative thoughts. Instead, you can contemplate the Presence of God right where you are. You're in the banquet house of the Lord. You can tune in to the Infinite this very moment. And you can *eat*, which means to meditate, absorb, and mentally digest the nourishing truths of God.

You can affirm: "Divine peace fills my soul, and the light of God illuminates my path." As you do so, you prepare a table in the Presence of the Lord. The bread you eat is God's idea of peace, love, and faith. Whenever you feel afraid or worried, mentally dwell on these truths and you'll experience harmony, health, and inspiration in your mind and heart.

You don't need flowers, music, incense, beads, or anything else to meditate. You also don't have to assume any particular posture or face east. You see, when you truly meditate, you need no props. You can meditate on a plane or train even when you don't know in which direction you're traveling. If you're relying on objects or external rituals, you're on the wrong track. Always start from the *inside,* practicing the Presence of God.

As you contemplate the great Divine truths, your blood pressure decreases and your every cell is filled with healing light. You're playing the melody of the One Who Forever Is, and every atom of your being dances to the rhythm of God's love.

⊰✣⊱

Dr. David Seabury was a noted psychologist who used the great healing techniques of Phineas Parkhurst Quimby. Dr. Seabury told me about a very wonderful woman whose husband was shot to death before her eyes. The shock of the incident left *her* paralyzed from the waist down, and the doctors didn't think that she'd ever walk again. However, Dr. Seabury told her, "Before the shooting, you rode horses, swam, and were athletic. Now this is what I want you to do. Even though you're paralyzed, imagine that you're on a horse. You can feel its mane and your feet in the stirrups. Really experience galloping through a field and jumping over a fence. Use all of your senses."

Dr. Seabury continued, "Now imagine that you're swimming. You can feel the chill of the water and your body moving through the currents. It's all real. Someone is congratulating you on crossing the lake as you dry off with a towel. Do these visualizations several times every day, and the time will come when you will walk."

For many weeks, she did this practice faithfully, using her imagination to fully experience riding and swimming. Then one day, Dr. Seabury told her that her only son had arranged to call her from South Africa at a specific time. The nurses were told to stay away from her room at the time of the call, and the telephone was put about 20 feet away from her bed.

When the phone rang and the woman realized that she was alone in her room, she got up to answer the call—a call of love. She loved her son and wanted to hear his voice. Dr. Seabury told me that after that, she was able to walk again and lived to be 90 years old.

There's nothing unusual about this story—such "miracles" are as common as breathing or eating. She'd suffered from a paralysis of her mind and didn't have a spinal injury of any kind. Spirit can't be paralyzed, and when she invested her mind in constructive thoughts, she had a complete healing.

What kind of thoughts are *you* investing in? If you're a doctor, you can say, "Every patient I touch is healed. Every medicine I prescribe is the right one, and I am guided to offer perfect treatments. The Miraculous Healing Intelligence works through me, for there is only One Power." When you pour your time and energy into thoughts of healing, you'll get wonderful results.

When you meditate, you can repeat the mantra *om*, which means the *I am*, the Living Spirit, and God. It isn't the sound of the mantra that's important but your understanding of its meaning, which is boundless love, absolute harmony, and complete joy. As you say *om*, you realize that all of these qualities are manifesting in your life and experience a great sense of peace and tranquility.

You need to remember that you're living in the objective world and are here to put your hands to the plow and bring forth the fruits of Spirit. You can't live in the clouds all of the time, and the results of your meditation must appear in your body, environment, home, relationships, work, and every other aspect of your life. Are you wrapped up in another world or are you manifesting peace, joy, abundance, security, and illumination? Are your thoughts blessing humanity?

We all need to bring the truths of God into form, experience, and event because faith without works is dead. If you meditate on the indescribable radiance of God, you bring forth beauty. And if you meditate on the peace of God, you plant the rich seeds of Divine harmony.

Dr. Emmet Fox, the author of *The Sermon on the Mount,* told a story about a patient of his who was full of resentment for bankers, investors, and other businesspeople. Dr. Fox advised him to go down to Wall Street and stand there for two hours every day, blessing every single person who came out of the brokers' offices and saying, "God's love fills your soul."

The man was reluctant in the beginning but went every day for the prescribed time. He subsequently had a miraculous healing. Why? Because he was meditating on love, and God's compassion filled his soul. As he dwelled on Divine love, it became a part of him and dissolved everything unlike itself, including sickness. This is the result of meditation.

Like all great scientists, Nikola Tesla brought forth his marvelous inventions through meditation. He was asked by a reporter one time how he came up with so many wonderful creations, including the monumental invention of the radio. He answered, "When I get an inkling of an idea, I close my eyes and become still. Then I say, 'Infinite Intelligence gave me this thought and provides all the details needed to bring it to fruition.' Every day I go back, sit quietly, and affirm that Infinite Intelligence fills in all the information and completes the design in my mind before I give it to the mechanics. There's no trial and error in my procedure."

Of course, this is what all great inventors do. They come up with ideas by meditating and quietly contemplating their reality. So, don't make a mystery of meditation because it's not an elusive process. You're always meditating on the eternal truths of God that are the same yesterday, today, and forever.

Someone who's angry and hateful quietly thinks up a scheme to kill the person he resents. As he continues to dwell on his destructive thoughts, they become a subconscious compulsion, and he carries out the murder. In the same way, people who contemplate love, peace, harmony, joy, inspiration, and illumination are compelled to express these qualities. An alcoholic who focuses on the love of God will be drawn to sobriety, and a person who suffers from chronic anxiety will be filled with peace.

If a singer is worried that she'll hit the wrong note, she can meditate and affirm: "God sings, speaks, and acts through me. I sing in majestic cadences that thrill the soul. I am confident and relaxed. The God who made my vocal chords sings through me. There is only one voice: the voice of the One Who Forever Is."

She prays in this manner three or four times a day, for a few minutes at a time. As she does so, she magnifies her desire in meditation, and it comes to fruition. After all, God is a great musician and singer, and the entire world is a song of the Divine.

Realize the great truth that detachment is the key to meditation. That is, we must completely separate ourselves from all worldly and false beliefs and instead focus silently upon the truths of the One Who Forever Is. Detachment doesn't mean that we give up our earthly possessions. Instead, it's about releasing the attachments that limit us to a human viewpoint in all matters.

You don't need to go to an ashram or a mountain retreat to meditate. You can do it in Times Square, Hollywood Boulevard, or anywhere else, for God dwells within you. You can commune with Him this very moment—on an airplane, in the silence of your own home, or wherever you may be. There's no mystery or trick you need to understand, and you don't have to pay $1,000 to take a meditation class. In fact, no one can teach you how to meditate. Simply go within, knowing that God or the Living Spirit abides within you. You'll find perfect and abiding peace. *Be still and know that I am God.*

We should meditate on beauty, love, and peace every day of our lives. We'll feel these qualities being resurrected in us. As we meditate daily on this inner radiance, realizing that the love, light, and glory of the Infinite are moving within us, we'll merge with the Divine Being within. For the first time, we'll discover that the sun, the moon, the stars, and the planets are within us. They're thoughts in our own consciousness and the dreams of the dreamer. God or Spirit is meditating on the mysteries of Himself. This inward journey ultimately leads us to what is true and to the realization of the Eternal One Who lives in the hearts of everyone.

When we meditate on the beauty and love of God, we realize that the petty irritations of daily life are inconsequential. Our soul is filled with the glory of the Infinite One, and the limitations and restrictions of our lives vanish. Greed, jealousy, discord, and other narrowing concepts that bind us to the wheel of pain disappear from our mind, forgotten in the joy of truth. We find that a happy mood lifts us up and puts us in touch with the universal mind of the Infinite. Meditation or the practice of the Presence of God restores harmony, beauty, grace, love, peace, joy, and wisdom to our every action. Spending half an hour a day meditating on our ideals, goals, and ambitions will transform us in a few months' time.

꙳✛꙳

Consistent meditation causes your mind to thrill as though touched by Divine harmony. A pulsating feeling pervades every part of you. Many experience it as a tingling sensation in the spinal area—as though the melody of God were being played on your spinal column. It's a wonderful feeling. Meditate on the One Who Forever Is in your own soul. You can dwell in the secret place in your mind where you walk and talk with Him.

As you're washing the dishes or driving to work, you can contemplate the great eternal truths of God and your love of music, art, and life. You can focus on the love of a mother who takes her crippled son all over the world to the spas and healing shrines so that he might experience a healing. You can dwell on the compassion of a father who works overtime and does everything possible to help his daughter. You can think about the soldier who sacrifices himself for his comrades, saying to himself, "I'm single and these other men are married and have children." He gives his life for them.

You can affirm: "God's love fills my soul." That's a magnificent mantra, and it's free and available to everyone. You can use it and experience boundless compassion, limitless joy, and absolute harmony permeating every atom of your being and mind. Divine love dissolves everything unlike itself, and you'll be inspired from On High. And remember that all of the love you can contemplate is but an infinitesimal fraction of the Infinite ocean of God's love.

In a Nutshell

Meditation means your inner conversation—what you say to yourself when you're all alone. That internal speech always manifests in your life because that's what you really believe.

As you drive along the road, you can contemplate the fact that God is guiding you now, right action reigns supreme, and Divine love fills your soul. God goes before you today and every day, making your path straight, perfect, and joyous.

If a negative thought comes into your mind, neutralize it with an affirmation such as, "God is love, and His peace fills my soul." A wonderful sense of calm and well-being should fill your soul when you meditate and pray.

You don't need to assume a particular posture or burn incense to meditate. You're always on a false path when you think that such rituals are necessary because that's starting from the outside. In India, they teach that you must start from the *inside,* the yoga of love. Then every single atom of your being will be transformed.

Meditation is the discipline of looking inward. You turn toward God and contemplate his truths from the highest perspective. It's a pilgrimage within. Realize that half an hour a day spent dwelling on your ideals, goals, and ambitions will transform you in a few months' time.

We should begin to meditate upon the beauty, glory, and profundity of the Eternal One every day. As we focus on the Divine within ourselves, we'll find an everlasting peace that stretches beyond the stars, time, and space.

When we think Divine thoughts, the petty irritations of life become inconsequential. Our soul is filled with the glory of Infinite Spirit, and the limitations and restrictions of our lives vanish.

Chapter Five

———•–•–•———

Do the Constellations Govern You?

*S*ince the earliest times, millions of people have believed in astrology. According to this so-called science, knowledge of the positions and movements of celestial bodies can help us understand and predict events in our lives. Astrology shouldn't be confused with *astronomy,* which is the scientific study of the universe beyond Earth. Astronomy makes no claims about anybody's life, fate, or destiny.

The fact is that you shouldn't give your allegiance to the stars and the planets but to the God Who created them. If you worship the constellations, you're honoring false gods, which goes against the biblical command: "Thou shalt have no other gods before me."

If you believe that you're doomed by some catastrophic configuration of the stars, that is your belief; and according to your belief it is done unto you. You become what you think about all day long, and you fashion your own destiny through your thoughts and feelings. Nothing is foreordained or predestined, and nothing can happen to you unless its mental equivalent is established in your subconscious. Your desires or ideas sink into your deeper mind to come forth as form, experience, and event.

God dwells within you and walks and talks in you. He's the Eternal Now and the Living Spirit within you. All good is available right now because God doesn't grow or expand. He's timeless and spaceless. Are you waiting for love? It's here already. Are you hoping for a cure for your disease? The Healing Presence is within you. Do you wish to have strength? The Almighty Power is within you, waiting for you to contact It. Joy, wealth, guidance, and everything else are within you now. You might as well claim your good and enjoy it immediately instead of waiting 50 years.

Many people—including some prominent individuals—still believe in astrology. They read their horoscopes daily in their local newspaper or consult astrologers about the problems they face. Indeed, some political leaders make decisions that affect their countries only after consulting an astrologer. Isn't that silly? If horoscopes had any meaning at all, every single person born under the same sign would have the same fate. To be sure, most of the information provided in horoscopes consists of broad generalities that could apply to anyone, but that in itself proves their banality.

The real danger of astrological predictions is their influence on the subconscious. Remember that the subconscious doesn't determine whether a suggestion is true or false, or helpful or harmful. It just accepts whatever idea you feed to it and manifests it in your life. For example, Carl P. told me, "There's a negative configuration of planets in my horoscope, and everything is going wrong." He was convinced that his acute loss of vision had been preordained by the stars even though his ophthalmologist thought that an emotional disturbance was the most likely cause of his declining vision.

In fact, as I talked with him, Carl revealed that he was full of resentment for his father-in-law and actually hated the sight of him. I explained that it's well known that mental and emotional factors can affect the eyes and play a role in disease—both in causing and curing it. I told him that he'd been decreeing his own blindness because the subconscious always takes us literally and always obeys the directives of the conscious mind.

The realization of what he was doing to himself became the cure. Carl's resentment and hostility disappeared as he affirmed lovingly: "I radiate love and goodwill to you [his father-in-law] and wish for you all the blessings of life. I see the Presence of God operating in you, through you, and all around you." He made a habit of saying this prayer, and his vision subsequently returned to normal.

If you believe that the constellations will cause you misfortune, it is done unto you as you believe. However, perhaps one of your associates down the hall doesn't believe in fate at all and prospers in a magnificent way. If you become intensely jealous of her success, you'll only bring further impoverishment into your life. In effect, you're saying, "She can become wealthy and climb the ladder of success, but I can't." You're putting someone else on a pedestal and demoting yourself. You're actually stealing from yourself and attracting further lack, misery, and limitation.

The zodiac is an imaginary line in the heavens. It's not a physical body and has no gravitational pull. Scientific thinkers wisely reject the idea that the 12 signs have any real meaning or influence. They don't give power to the effect but to the One Cause or God. Don't give your allegiance to constellations in the sky—to outlines of a goat, bull, or fish. Set your heart upon God and not upon external forms. We *all* have the "12 powers" of the signs, including imagination, love, and discernment. Furthermore, we possess all of the attributes and qualities of God. We're here to develop these and become true disciples of the Divine.

Infinite Intelligence is love and seeks to express Itself as harmony, beauty, peace, joy, abundance, and security. That's the tendency of life. God was never born and will never die. He's the Living Spirit within us.

Shakespeare wrote: "The fault, dear Brutus, is not in our stars, But in ourselves, that we are underlings." The only power is in your own *consciousness,* which means your *I am,* your awareness, and the Living Spirit of God within you. Your state of consciousness is the way you think, feel, and believe and whatever you give mental consent to. There's no other cause or power in this world, and it is done unto you as you believe. You should, therefore, believe in the goodness and love of God and know that what is true of God is true of you. *I have come that they might have life, and have it more abundantly.*

Two professors who are friends of mine had their astrological charts done for $50 each. At my suggestion, they agreed not to read them and to let me hang onto them for a year lest they fill their subconscious minds with negative suggestions. During this time, I thoroughly explained the law of life to them: *As a man thinketh, so is he.* That's the universal law and the basis of all religions throughout the world. We each shape our own destiny through our habitual thoughts and feelings.

I also let them know that even though their subconscious minds may have been polluted with negativity and false beliefs in the past, they could now change by identifying with the eternal verities. They could charge their mental and spiritual batteries regularly and systematically by contemplating the truths of God, which transcend all astrological charts.

Both of my friends practiced constructive thinking throughout the year. Each morning and evening, they read from a book of meditations that I gave them and saturated their minds with Divine truth, neutralizing and obliterating all the self-defeating patterns of the deeper mind. As they planted harmony, beauty, love, peace, and right action in their subconscious, they activated these powers of God in their lives.

At the end of the year, my friends examined their horoscopes in my office and laughed out loud because their astrological charts contained predictions that had never come to pass. In fact, although financial losses and accidents were indicated, they experienced success and health instead. Both men had prospered and been promoted at their respective colleges. Had they read their horoscopes earlier, they likely would have impressed negative suggestions upon their subconscious minds and experienced all kinds of misfortune.

The incredible power of suggestion is that no matter what you accept, your subconscious brings it to pass—whether it's good or bad.

☙✝❧

I've known psychics without any knowledge of astrology who could read the past, present, and future with extraordinary acumen, revealing the tendencies and characteristics of individuals. Some used a deck of cards and made predictions with amazing accuracy. Others used their clairvoyant or clairaudient gifts.

The entire psychic process is about tapping into someone's subconscious. The psychic gets into a passive, receptive state and enters into a rapport with your deeper mind, seeing your plans, purposes, fears, dreams, divorces, and whatever else is in your subconscious. You've revealed everything to the psychic everything before he or she tells you anything.

-<+>-

If there's any validity at all to astrological predictions, it's the result of the beliefs of the race or mass mind. Down through the ages, the race mind has given power to the constellations and astrological signs, believing that they exert an influence over us. All of us—more than six billion people—are affected by the beliefs of the collective unconscious unless we can free our mind through scientific prayer or the contemplation of the truths of God from the highest standpoint. Then we'll neutralize the toxic effluvia of the mass mind. We're all in a psychic sea and need to actively reject negative global beliefs.

-<+>-

It's wrong to predict evil for others. When you do so, you're actually drawing misfortune to *yourself.* Furthermore, you're contaminating other people's minds, planting the seeds of fear and worry. Would you want someone to prophesy doom in your life or predict that you're going to be shot or die? I don't think you would, so let's rid ourselves of these superstitious notions. Instead, use the power of the mind to pray for others to prosper. When you do so, you're also praying for your own abundance because your thought is creative. Affirm that the healing love of God flows through everybody now.

-<+>-

Pat went to the astrologer and said, "I'll give you $1,000 if you'll tell me where I'm going to die." The astrologist asked, "What on earth do you want to know that for?" Pat answered, "So I'll never go near the place." You see, these things can be funny, too.

We're now slowly moving into the Age of Aquarius, which, according to predictions, is supposed to be an era of great destruction. Well, death is a prelude to something better. We must die to what we are before we can become what we long to be. We must die to sickness to experience health, wholeness, and vitality. We must let go of the cursed idea of poverty and realize that God's riches are all around us. The Bible says that God generously gives us everything to enjoy—yet so many people are poor. They're poor in faith, love, goodwill, and knowledge of the laws of mind and the way of the Spirit.

It's time to get rid of old superstitions and beliefs, including the idea that we're sinners in the hands of an angry God or that there's a hell for those who disobey God's will. We're here to plant a garden of harmony, beauty, love, right action, and abundance. When we activate these principles within us, we're able to give encouragement, guidance, and love to others. We're also able to impart the laws of mind to our children and give light to all people everywhere.

We're all brought up with certain beliefs, opinions, and attitudes toward life. Although we're each conditioned differently in our youth, nothing is fated because we can change our lives by tuning in to the Infinite and claiming that what is true of God is true of us. As we think, speak, and act from the standpoint of the Infinite Presence and Power, we'll cast a spiritual horoscope for ourselves based upon wisdom, truth, and Divine law and order.

A young actress who'd been in a serious car wreck told me, "I knew that I was going have an accident. I read my horoscope, and it said that Neptune was positioned to cause me trouble. I saw that and got scared." In fact, she brought the accident upon herself. As Job said, "The thing which I greatly feared has come upon me." The truth is that Neptune is harmless and can't hurt anyone. There's only *One* Power: God.

Sorcery, witchcraft, and voodoo are all based on the power of suggestion and are used by people who are ignorant of real spiritual power. You have the ability to reject the negative suggestions and predictions of others. Walk in the consciousness of God's love and radiate compassion and goodwill to everyone. You'll gradually build up immunity against the false beliefs of the world.

⊱✠⊰

No matter who you are or where you are, and regardless of the sign you were born under, you can call upon the Spiritual Presence and Power that created the universe. Nothing can oppose or thwart It. If you open your mind and heart to receive, It will answer you and restore your soul. However, if you believe that Saturn is working against you, then the Infinite can't work through you. Rely upon the Spirit within, and then all things will become new and all of your obstacles and difficulties will dissolve.

In a Nutshell

Nothing is foreordained or predestined, and nothing can happen to you unless its mental equivalent is established in your subconscious. You fashion your own future with your thoughts and feelings.

The zodiac is an imaginary line in the heavens. It's not a physical body and has no gravitational pull. Scientific thinkers wisely reject the idea that the 12 signs have any real meaning or influence. They don't give power to the effect but to the One Cause or God. Set your heart upon Him and not upon external forms.

The real danger of astrological predictions is their influence on the subconscious. Remember that the subconscious doesn't determine whether a suggestion is true or false, or helpful or harmful. It just accepts whatever idea you feed to it and manifests it in your life.

It's time to discard the old idea that we're sinners in the hands of an angry God or that there's a hell waiting for those who disobey God's will. On the contrary, Divine Spirit is love and seeks to express Itself as harmony, beauty, peace, joy, abundance, and security.

People who try to use black magic and lay a curse on you are ignorant. They don't know what they're talking about. When you see these individuals in their true light, their influence falls away. There is only *One* Power, and you can use It constructively to neutralize all negative suggestions.

Chapter Six

Speaking in Tongues:
What It Really Means

*I*n the second book of Acts, it says: "And when the day of Pentecost was fully come, they [the apostles] were all with one accord in one place. And suddenly there came a sound from heaven as of a rushing mighty wind, and it filled all the house where they were sitting. And there appeared unto them cloven tongues like as of fire, and it sat upon each of them. And they were all filled with the Holy Ghost, and began to speak with other tongues, as the Spirit gave them utterance."

Pentecost is a feast that takes place on the seventh Sunday after Easter to celebrate the visit by the Holy Ghost to the apostles. However, to understand the true meaning of Pentecost, we have to understand that the stories of the Bible are figurative and symbolic. The phrase "they were all with one accord in one place" means that the apostles focused all their attention on God within—the Infinite Being Who is boundless love, unlimited joy, and absolute harmony. Then they heard the *rushing wind,* which represents the movement of the Spirit through our mind and heart and is the answer to our prayer.

The apostles merged with the One Spirit and experienced the illumination of pure compassion. Then they began to "speak with other tongues," which means using the universal language of love, peace, harmony, joy, goodwill, inspiration, and guidance. We all understand this idiom of the kingdom of God within. It lifts people up and is sweet to the soul.

When you make a habit of praying and communing with the Infinite, you'll find the exhilaration of the Spirit animating and inspiring you. As you gather your thoughts and feelings "with one accord" and focus on God Who dwells within, your entire being will be transfused with Spirit. You'll also feel compelled to express truth in a new way. You've stirred up the gift of God within you and in your joy will speak in other tongues—in the languages of compassion, peace, and abundance.

You've entered into the light referred to as *the promised land* in the Bible. It's the realization of your heart's desire and the answer to your prayers. If you experience a wonderful healing, that's the promised land. It has no geographical borders whatsoever. You're living in this heaven when you're expressing harmony, enthusiasm, and prosperity.

The *apostles* represent the faculties of your mind. In prayer, you gather your faculties and withdraw from the objective world and the evidence of your senses. You tune in to the Infinite Healing Presence within you and dwell on your ideal or the solution to your problem. In this quiet, receptive state, claim that the Almighty Power is now flowing through you. Feel the movement of the Spirit through you in the same way that you feel the warmth of the sun. This peaceful, confident mood is the mighty wind or the Spirit of God that fills your mind.

Sometimes when they're in a trance state, mediums will speak in various languages. They can do this because the subjective mind knows all of the dialects, since these are recorded in the universal or collective subconscious. Their subconscious is one with the universal subconscious and can tap into this store of knowledge. However, speaking in foreign tongues when one is in a hypnotic trance is no indication of spiritual enlightenment or illumination.

I was told about a 25-year-old woman who could neither read nor write. However, one day she was seized with a fever and began speaking Latin, Greek, and Hebrew in very pompous tones and with a most distinct enunciation. Her physician did some research and discovered that when this woman was a child, she'd been charitably taken care of by an old Protestant pastor. It appears that he had a habit of walking up and down the halls in his house, reading aloud from rabbinical writings and Greek and Latin works. The doctor was able to verify that the things the woman was saying were from the passages she'd heard the pastor read in her childhood.

It's easy to understand how this woman could suddenly speak foreign languages. When she developed a fever, her conscious mind was in abeyance and allowed her subconscious memories to be released. Thousands of similar cases are recorded and are easily explained without resorting to claims that people "speaking in tongues" are being possessed by disembodied spirits. Remember that the memory of everything that has ever transpired is inscribed on our subconscious minds.

In his work *Ancient Metaphysics,* Lord Monboddo tells the story of the Countess of Levalle. After she gave birth to one of her children, the nurse attending to her heard her talking in her sleep in a foreign language. The nurse, who was from Brittany, France, immediately recognized the language as one of the dialects of her country and understood what her patient was saying. However, when the countess awoke, and what she'd said in her sleep was repeated to her, she didn't understand a single syllable.

As it turns out, the Countess of Levalle had been born in Brittany and nursed in a family where only Breton was spoken. So, in her infancy she'd known only that local language. But when she went to live with her parents, she had no opportunity to use it. Breton had been recorded in her subconscious, but her knowledge of it only emerged when her conscious mind was asleep.

──✠──

Everything that you saw, read, or heard as a child is recorded indelibly and infallibly in your subconscious. Your conscious mind may have forgotten about an event, but if you were put in a hypnotic state and told, "Describe your fourth birthday and who was there," you'd be able to say all the names of the guests, what gifts you'd received, and what kind of cake was served. If we checked with your parents, we'd discover that your description was absolutely accurate. Your subconscious has a perfect memory of that birthday that you can tap into when the conscious mind is in abeyance.

Is there anything that isn't known in your deeper mind? No, all things are known. As the Bible says: "Before they call, I will answer; And while they are still speaking, I will hear."

──✠──

You can remove your attention from any negative thoughts and decisively focus your mind on your goal or ideal. In this quiet, receptive state, you realize that the Almighty Power always responds to your thoughts and brings your desires to pass. It vitalizes and restores your entire being. Feel the Healing Spirit move through you in a magnificent, wonderful way. This process is a form of prayer.

As you continue to faithfully pray like this, the answers will come, day will break, and the shadows will fade away. Your old state of consciousness will be obliterated as your new conditions manifest in your life. In other words, you must die to what you are before you can become what you long to be.

A man who's very ill prays: "The Healing Power is flowing through me, and God walks and talks in me." He imagines himself back in the office, doing all the things he would do if he were well. He realizes that Divine Spirit moves through his focal point of attention. As he continues to pray faithfully, he cooperates with his doctor and blesses him. Then the day comes when the man is able to walk, resume his work, and live with a great sense of well-being. *I am the Lord that healeth thee.*

Our words should radiate peace, love, and harmony to everyone. In other words, we should boldly affirm that the Infinite Spirit thinks, speaks, and acts through everybody we meet. Their subconscious mind will be aware of the light and the love we're imparting, and they'll be lifted up and made whole. We're speaking in the language of love, faith, and peace; and it inspires them.

The biblical story of Babel describes how at one time, there was only one language that everyone could use and understand. However, then God came and scattered the people living in the land of Shinar all around the world and confused their language so that they couldn't understand one another.

In this allegory, the cacophony of different languages represents the fact that the ways of the Infinite can never be fully understood by humankind. You can pray and have faith that you'll be answered, but you can never know how the answer will come or what it will be. As the Bible says: "As the heavens are higher than the earth, so are my ways higher than your ways, and my thoughts than your thoughts."

Dr. Alexis Carrel, a winner of the Nobel Prize in Physiology or Medicine, points out the marvelous effects produced by prayer. He describes seeing a malignant tumor shrivel to a scar before his eyes. In addition, he has observed cases in which the power of prayer caused wounds and lesions to heal in anywhere from a few seconds to a few hours, with all pathological symptoms disappearing. Through prayer, Carrel notes, the natural processes of organic repair become extremely accelerated.

The healing of growths, tumors, and burns are due to nothing more than the descent of the "tongues of fire" mentioned in the second book of Acts. The *fire* is God's love, peace, and light that dissolves everything unlike itself.

When you tune in to the Infinite Healing Power with faith, expectancy, and an active imagination, the influx of Spirit will respond, permeating your entire being and restoring you to wholeness, beauty, and perfection.

The Divine Presence is sometimes called *energy* by scientists. It can be used in many different ways, but it's all Infinite Spirit. You can use this energy to study, create, or walk . . . or to get angry and worked up, which is destructive to your tissues and organs. Some people spend most of their time eating and drinking—and it shows in their bodies. Others devote all of their attention to acquiring material goods and other physical pleasures, which is destructive and clouds their spirituality. You must decide how *you* are going to use your energy.

We're told that love never fails, yet there are prophets of doom everywhere. Some predict that an earthquake in California will cause the state to sink into the sea. Others foresee a nuclear holocaust, global famine, overpopulation, and the end of the world. Consider how often these prognosticators have had to eat crow.

If you look back on your life, most of the things you worried about never happened. But your anxiety depleted your vitality and robbed you of discernment and good judgment. Perhaps it also brought on ulcers and other illnesses.

Decide now to speak in a new tongue. Become a prophet of God and dwell in the Secret Place of the Lord. Abide in the shadow of the Almighty. You'll say, "God is my refuge and my fortress. In Him, I will trust. And the angels of God watch over me lest I dash my foot against a stone." The angels, of course, are the inspiration, guidance, and wisdom of God that anoint your intellect and light your path.

You're now speaking in the language of love, faith, and confidence in the One Power. Trust this Power and believe in It and you'll lead a charmed life. You'll be impervious to all harm. Nothing can hurt you because you're always watched over by the Infinite Presence. Turn your thoughts to God and ignore all of the predictions about disaster and the end of the world.

Focus upon what God has said instead of letting your mind dwell on the things you fear. Contemplate the fact that God is guiding you and that Divine love goes before you, making your path straight and joyous.

Calm your thoughts and emotions by contemplating God, Who is your light and salvation. The Almighty Power guides you, watches over you, and sustains you. The Bible says: "Fear not, for I am with you; Be not dismayed, for I am your God. I will strengthen you . . ."

Love means loyalty to the One Power, the only Cause and Substance. Give your allegiance to this Presence, and not to any created thing—to no man, woman, child, circumstance, or event. The Bible says: "You shall love the Lord your God with all your heart, with all your soul, and with all your mind."

Read these words and dwell upon them. The Almighty Power is within you. It will lift you up, heal you, and set you on the high road to happiness, freedom, and peace of mind. *The Lord is my light and my salvation; whom shall I fear?*

When it appears that someone is undermining you or lying about you, or you're faced with a lawsuit, affirm: "In God I have put my trust. I am not afraid of what any human can do to me, for He thinks, speaks, and acts through me. One with God is a majority, and if God is for me, who can be against me?" As you dwell on these truths, your fear will go away. You'll be speaking in the language of confidence, love, and joy.

Your conscious mind can be likened to the ship captain who directs the crew in the engine room. He doesn't steer the vessel himself but issues orders. The sailors don't decide whether or not to do what he commands; they just carry out the directives. If the orders are bad, the ship might hit an iceberg.

In this analogy, the *crew* is your subconscious. You're constantly giving mental orders to your deeper mind. What language are you using? Are you speaking in fear, anxiety, gloom, and sickness? Or are you using the language of faith, confidence, love, goodwill, vitality, and wholeness?

Enthrone Divine ideas in your conscious mind. As you focus directly on the eternal truths of life, you'll begin to speak in a new, melodious language. It will be the voice of wisdom and joy, and your words will be sweet to the soul.

Jewish scholars believe in the coming of a messiah who will bring us a perfect world. Christians, on the other hand, believe that Jesus was the messiah and preach that the perfect world will come when he returns. In both traditions, *messiah* is a metaphor for the ideal world. The second coming isn't about some superbeing descending from the clouds with angels and a harp; it's the realization that God's love, peace, harmony, beauty, and inspiration are already in your own mind and heart. These qualities and attributes of God were never born and will never die. They're within you, and you can resurrect them now. When you let love, peace, and beauty into your mind and heart, that's the second coming.

How could there be a literal second coming? The Divine Presence can't come or go because It's omnipresent and therefore within you. Spirit was never born and will never die . . . It has always been here. *Ye are gods; and all of you are children of the most High.*

Don't wait to experience God's love. It's already within you, and you might as well enjoy it now instead of on some future date. Why not feel the peace of God this moment instead of waiting 50 years?

You know very well that if the fortune-tellers of the world could accurately predict which stocks and bonds would go up in value, they'd be rolling in wealth. Are they actually millionaires? Wake up! You can already foretell your own future, because according to your belief, it is done unto you. *Whatsoever ye shall ask in prayer, believing, ye shall receive.* Believe that God is guiding you and believe in Divine goodness in the land of the living.

Many people talk about *Armageddon* but don't even know the meaning of this term that's described in the book of Revelation. It's vital to remember that the Bible is allegorical and that you're not supposed to take the stories literally. I wrote a book called *Pray Your Way Through It* that interprets the true meaning of Revelation and the so-called end of the world.

Don't believe in the prognosticators of doom and gloom. Believe instead in the goodness and love of the Lord. He is pure compassion and can't do anything destructive. Know that Divine law and order govern your life and that God is prospering you beyond your fondest dreams. As the Bible says: "God is our refuge and strength, A very present help in trouble. Therefore we will not fear, Even though the earth be removed, And though the mountains be carried into the midst of the sea . . ."

Dwell on these truths instead of the negative predictions of the media and you'll live above the mass mind. The God Presence is within you and is waiting for you to call upon It. Your future is created by your habitual thoughts, which manifest on the screen of space. When you know that, you begin to speak in the language of faith and love.

It's not adequate to say, "I believe in God." Instead, ask yourself: *What do I really believe is true about the Infinite Presence within me?* Your answer is the most important thing in your life and must come from your heart. If you have a false, superstitious concept of the Divine, there will be chaos and confusion in your life.

Begin to believe that God is the Omnipotent Life Principle within you. He created you from a cell and possesses boundless love, complete perfection, and absolute harmony. He's the only Power, Cause, and Substance. He's within you, and what's true of God must therefore be true of you. Begin to know in your heart that you possess all of the love, intelligence, truth, and beauty of God. Everything in your life will change, you'll go from glory to glory, and all of the shadows will flee. You'll be speaking the language of faith.

It's foolish to believe that you must reincarnate or come back again and again in order to work out some karma or suffer for your misdeeds in a former life. This belief is a sort of opiate that dulls the mind and prevents spiritual development. It's also a complete contradiction of the teachings of the Bible and the ancient wisdom. Finally, it's contrary to natural law and can't be true.

The biblical story of the blind man argues against a belief in karma. According to this allegory, when a disciple saw a blind man, he asked Jesus, "Master, who did sin, this man, or his parents, that he was born blind?" Jesus responded, "Neither hath this man sinned, nor his parents: but that the works of God should be made manifest in him." Then Jesus commanded the blind man to wash in the pool of Siloam. The man did so, and his eyesight was restored.

Washing in the Bible means casting aside all the prevalent and false beliefs of the times, such as thinking that blindness is caused by sins in a former life. And it was the day of the Sabbath when Jesus led the blind man to see. The *Sabbath* has nothing to do with the days of the week. It means your conviction or the point of acceptance, when your prayer is answered. *"Come now, and let us reason together,"* saith the Lord. *"Though your sins be as scarlet, they shall be as white as snow; though they be red like crimson, they shall be as wool."*

⊱✝⊰

The law of cause and effect is a timeless principle. If you've been misusing the law, you can change your mental attitude and thereby transform the events that unfold in your life. When you use the law wisely and constructively, we call it *God.* When you use the law maliciously, ignorantly, or stupidly, we call it *evil,* because we inflict all manner of suffering upon ourselves by misdirecting the law of our lives.

⊱✝⊰

Our children grow up in the image and the likeness of the dominant mental and emotional climate of their home. Therefore, realize that they are God's children. Know that the love, light, and glory of God surrounds them and affirm that they're growing in wisdom, strength, beauty, grace, and happiness. God only wants to heal us. He loves us, and His peace fills our soul. He is with us now and forevermore.

In a Nutshell

Everyone understands the universal language of love and the meaning of a gentle smile. Decide now to speak in this new tongue. Become a prophet of God and dwell in the Secret Place of the Almighty. You'll say of the Lord, "He is my refuge and my fortress. My God, in Him I will trust."

Remember that the subconscious records everything that's ever happened to you and everything you've ever known. When the conscious mind is in abeyance because of conditions such as fever or hypnosis, all of the treasures of the subconscious are instantly available. You may marvel at this wonderful gift of the mind.

Whenever you remove your attention from a negative condition or thought and place it upon something far more godlike, the destructive idea dies and makes space for the resurrection of good. In other words, you must die to what you are before you can become what you long to be.

Our words should radiate peace, love, and harmony to everyone. We should boldly affirm that the Infinite Spirit thinks, speaks, and acts through us and that all those listening to us are inspired and made whole. Then we're speaking in the language of love, faith, and upliftment. The people around us will be subconsciously aware of the indefinable Divine essence that permeates our words. This is the perfume of the gods.

Focus on what God has said instead of letting your mind dwell on the things you fear. Contemplate the fact that God is guiding you and that Divine love goes before you, making your path straight, peaceful, and joyous. Remember that the things we worry about most almost never happen but that all of our anxiety wreaks havoc in our bodies and lives.

You can contemplate Psalm 23 to combat your fears. Say to yourself: *Yea, though I walk through the shadow of death, I will fear no evil: For You are with me; Your rod and Your staff, they comfort me.* Dwell on these truths and repeat them to yourself. You can say them out aloud—slowly, quietly, and reverently. As you do so, your fears will melt away. You'll be speaking in a new language of faith, love, and trust in the Almighty Power.

Believe in the goodness and love of God. Since God is pure compassion, He can't do anything unloving. Know that Divine law and order govern your life and that Infinite Spirit prospers you beyond your fondest dreams.

Chapter Seven

A New Look at Reincarnation

I believe that the time has come in the field of mental and spiritual law, and in our thinking and practice, to address the misunderstood subject of reincarnation, which is believed in by great numbers of people in many parts of the world. I've written about it in two of my other books: *Great Bible Truths for Human Problems* and *Psychic Perception: The Magic of Extrasensory Power.*

According to the theory of reincarnation, we continue to come back to Earth to live new lives until we become perfect and return no more. Well, of course we all know that repetition doesn't always lead to growth. You could come back a thousand or a million times, but it won't necessarily make you spiritually enlightened. In fact, growth only takes place in the timeless space where you ascend the hill of God. Furthermore, anyone can merge with the Infinite Presence at any time. For example, even murderers who have a hunger to become one with Spirit can claim the love, peace, and harmony of God. Then as they saturate their minds with the eternal truths, they're compelled toward renewal. They can't repeat their old mistakes and they become holy.

God is the Eternal Now Who is never born and will never die. He's the Living Spirit Almighty within each of us and is whole, perfect, and complete. It follows that what's true of God is also true of us. This means that we need to let go of the idea that we must continually be reborn in the three-dimensional plane. We shouldn't surrender to the mistaken beliefs of those who fail to see that the Timeless One is within us and that we're not victims of the past.

Our Savior—the One Presence, Power, and Substance—is within us now. Surely you don't say, "Someday I'll get a healing. Someday I'll have love in my life. Someday I'll find peace of mind"! The God of peace fills you right now, so why wait to experience Him? You might as well claim Divine joy and harmony today instead of waiting a few more decades.

Einstein brought us to the temple gate by toppling the false gods of time and space and revealing that time has no existence apart from our own mind or consciousness. He illustrated his theory of relativity by observing that if we put our hand on a hot stove for a minute, it feels like an hour; but if we spend an hour with an attractive man or woman, it seems like a minute. In short, time is a state of mind and has no beginning or end. God is the Eternal Now, and today is the day of salvation. After all, in the Bible, Jesus says: "Assuredly, I say to you, today you will be with me in paradise." He doesn't say that we can be in heaven tomorrow or next year but *today*.

In biblical times and still today, people wait for the messiah to come. But the messiah is *within* you. It's the God Presence that fills your mind and body. This Presence was never born and will never die, and It's instantly available to you right now. Peace, love, beauty, inspiration, healing, and power are always within you. *Then you will*

*call upon Me and go and pray to Me, and I will listen to you. And you will
seek Me and find Me, when you search for Me with all your heart.*

By believing in the theory of reincarnation, you fall from spiritual grace. Your subconscious belief that you must come back to
atone for the sins of your past lives holds you in spiritual bondage
and indicates that you have a guilt complex. The truth is that God
doesn't seek to punish you, but when you believe in your subconscious that He does, you bring it to pass. Therefore, you're keeping
yourself in slavery.

The Bible says that God gave the son of man the authority to
judge. The *son* represents your mind, which has all the power to
decide. Therefore, begin now to extinguish all the fires of karma
and purgatory by having true faith and conviction in God's love
and beauty here and now. Refuse to be satisfied by anything but
the promised land of spiritual reality.

In scientific circles, it's customary to discard yesterday's dis-
proved theories and outdated ideas. With great courage and without hesitation, brilliant thinkers jettison concepts that have been
shown to be false, even if people held them to be true for hundreds
of years. Likewise, you must throw out the old notion that we reach
enlightenment through a slow, laborious process of reincarnation.
Arrive at the hour of decision in your own mind and open yourself
to the influx of the Holy Spirit. As Jesus told his disciples, "The
kingdom of God is within you." Peace already is! Illumination
already is! You can claim them now, for the kingdom is already
complete and present.

Free yourself from psychologically imprisoning ideas about time. Become a child of God and leap for joy beneath the stars of love, truth, and beauty, which are timeless and everlasting. Light up the heavens of your own mind. Every time you pray, you're spiritually reincarnated. You've had hundreds of rebirths since you were born, because you've continued to bring more and more God Presence into your life. You're not the same person you were 20 years ago, 5 years ago, or even 1 year ago.

True reincarnation is the birth of God in your mind and heart. You can become intoxicated with the Divine right now and experience an ever-increasing measure of Spirit. Life is growth, expansion, and newness; and you can't be less tomorrow than you are today. If you're in the eighth grade, you can't be sent back to elementary school. Life doesn't go backward or tarry with yesterday. It moves from glory to glory, strength to strength, and wisdom to wisdom. There's no limit to your illumination, for that would be contrary to natural law.

According to Hindu scripture, Spirit is never born and will never die, so there's no reason to grieve for your loved ones who've passed on to the next dimension. What's true on one plane of life is true on all planes, and your friends and family members will continue to learn and grow. There are teachers in the next phase of existence just as there are on Earth, for our journey is ever onward, upward, and godward.

In fact, our loved ones are all around us, separated by their different rate of vibration. The child who dies in the womb lives forever and is a grace note in the symphony of all creation. This blessed soul continues to grow and expand in the next plane.

In the Hindu and Buddhist religions, *karma* is the sum of a person's actions. They teach that the fruits of one's deeds create all past, present, and future experiences. In short, karma is the cycle of death and rebirth that an individual endures until he or she achieves spiritual liberation or enlightenment.

In simple terms, karma is really the law of cause and effect: Whatever is impressed on the subconscious is expressed as experiences, events, circumstances, and conditions. However, in contrast with karma, in the law of mind there's no time or space, and what you're manifesting can be changed immediately when you change your thoughts. You don't have to wait until the next life for transformation. You can begin at this very moment to feed your subconscious with life-giving thoughts of harmony, happiness, and love; and you'll receive an automatic response of joy and blessings. You'll no longer be a victim but will become a victor.

As you saturate your subconscious with positive images and thoughts, you'll gradually obliterate all the old, negative habits of your deeper mind. By filling your subconscious with the eternal truths, you neutralize and push out everything that's unlike God.

No matter what your problems are or how difficult they appear, they're always caused by a group of negative thoughts and emotions lodged in your subjective depths. You can begin to clean and purify these recesses of your deeper mind by pouring in the waters of life and truth. You can visualize this process by imagining a pail of filthy water. If you add distilled water to it—even drop by drop—you'll eventually have clear, pure water that you can drink.

It doesn't matter if your water has been dirty for 50 years; you can always start to transform it. You can do this by taking time in the morning and evening to joyously affirm that the Infinite ocean of life, love, truth, and beauty is flowing through you, cleansing and healing your entire being. The wholeness and peace of God reign supreme in your mind and heart, and you sing the song of glory.

⛧

Imagine that you'd misused the principles of mathematics for 20 years, perhaps causing yourself a lot of trouble and financial loss. Obviously, the rules of addition and subtraction don't hold a grudge against you; and the minute you learn how to apply them, you'll automatically get beneficial results.

Your mind is also a principle that doesn't hang on to resentments. When you dwell on what's good, positive outcomes always manifest; and when you think negatively, misery is always the result.

⛧

Ernest Holmes told me that when he studied with Emma Curtis Hopkins, she related a wonderful true story that took place in a state penal institution. This is the essence of her account: A man convicted of murder was sentenced to be hanged. During the interim between his sentence and his scheduled execution, he became aware of the love and truth of God. A young girl gave him a pamphlet in which it was written: "The Lord is too pure to behold inequity and treachery." The prisoner began to consider this passage from all angles and saw that God is deliverance; He doesn't condemn, judge, or punish us. We only hurt ourselves by misusing His law. The man recognized the great truth of God and saw that His love and mercy are everlasting.

To the great perplexity of the officers of the law, when the condemned man was led to the gallows, the platform that would ordinarily tip at the slightest weight became firm when he steppe upon it. They tried to carry out his execution repeatedly but to no avail. Finally, the man was granted his freedom.

Had his adoration of the Divine and the transformation of his heart caused his life to be saved? The love of God indeed surpasses all understanding. The Almighty's wonders and blessings are unlimited. The convict had emancipated his consciousness, entered into the glorious liberty of God, and become a free man.

The law of karma is only inexorable as long as you don't pray or meditate on the truths of God. If you have an intense desire to become a new person in God and fill your mind with the great eternal truths, you *will* be transformed. According to the law of the subconscious, you'll be compelled to express your inner assumptions and beliefs and will no longer repeat your previous errors. You rise above karma and wipe out the unpleasant consequences of past mistakes. No matter how awful the crime or offense, it can be expunged from your mind as you imbue your heart with Divine love and grace.

If you believe that God is punishing you for your past mistakes, you have a false concept of the Divine. Furthermore, if you continue to maintain such a superstitious belief about God, chaos and confusion will reign in your life. Ask yourself: *What do I really believe is true of the Infinite Presence within me?* Your answer is the most important guiding force in your life.

Begin to believe that God is all-wise and possesses boundless love, absolute harmony, and pure joy. What's true of God is always true of you as well, for He dwells within you. God and all of His manifestations are one and the same. As you develop faith in the Infinite Presence, everything in your life will improve, including your relationships, finances, health, and creativity.

⊨✝⊨

Are the sins of the parents really visited upon their children? Well, "sins" are really the misuse of the laws of mind. Mothers and fathers may commit the sin of holding fears, superstitions, and false beliefs in their subconscious. Unfortunately, they transmit these destructive mental states to their children. For example, a father can instill a fear of God in his child by communicating his belief that He punishes sinners and rules the world with cruel caprice. As a result, the child grows up believing in a wrathful God—a sort of despot in the skies.

On the other hand, as you begin to realize the omnipotence of the Spirit within and the power of your own thought, you can pass on this incredible knowledge to your children. As you enthrone thoughts of peace, love, joy, and wholeness in your subconscious, it will respond by opening the windows of heaven and pouring out blessings until there's not enough room to receive them all.

⊨✝⊨

Judge Troward pointed out that we're all immersed in the mass or race consciousness. Today about six billion people make up that one mind, and its negative influence can be extremely strong. If we don't do our own thinking, the mass mind will do it for us and cause havoc and pain in our lives. However, if we focus on creating positive thoughts, we begin to transform the race consciousness.

⊨✝⊨

When a cruel dictator appears in the world, he's never a reincarnation of Genghis Khan or any other tyrant who lived before. He's actually an embodiment of the state of consciousness of his country or region. What happens is that as children grow up, they learn about the wars and conflicts in which their country has been involved. In some instances, they're taught to hate their neighboring nations. Some of these kids develop rage about what has happened in the past and begin to read avidly about the crimes, atrocities, and acts of violence that have occurred. Negative thoughts fill their subconscious and must ultimately be expressed in the world. A dictator is a state of consciousness that manifests in the external plane.

Children grow up in the image and the likeness of the dominant mental, emotional, and spiritual climate of their home and school. If parents and teachers understood the laws of mind and taught the eternal verities, the next generation wouldn't be filled with beggars, outcasts, tyrants, and criminals.

By teaching young people who they really are—by showing them the Way, the Truth, and the Light—we can build a heaven on Earth and prevent the development of the undesirable states of consciousness that are perpetuated by prejudices, racial hatreds, and fear of the unknown. We need to teach them about the magnificent accomplishments of the poets, scientists, and illumined seers, for children tend to emulate the ideals that are presented to them.

The great and wise thinkers have taught that you can experience illumination or the magnificent awakening to your Divinity here and now. If it doesn't happen today, it will eventually as you raise your rate of vibration to a high level through the contemplation of the Presence and Power of God within. In this lovely meditative state, you'll gradually appropriate more and more of the attributes and qualities of God. As you continue this practice, you'll experience a great expansion of consciousness. The day will come when you'll melt away all of your inhibitions, fears, false beliefs, and doubts and know that you are God.

This transformation can take place in a flash, just as water can instantly be converted into steam. For instance, sometimes we hear news reports about people who've been paralyzed for years leaping out of bed when their house catches fire. They're suddenly healed and escape into the street. In other emergencies, women have been able to lift cars off of their children or husbands to save their lives. Where does this power come from? It's within them . . . and within each of us. But we don't have to be facing a dire situation to stir up our inner God Presence. We can resurrect Divine Power and Intelligence through silent contemplation of our soul. God abides in the silence and transmits His truth. When we unite with the Infinite, we're in union with the Intelligence beyond time and space, where we find the strength and peace that surpass all understanding.

I've seen women in India and elsewhere in the world look into the eyes of their newborns and say "What sin brought you back to me?" The belief behind this statement is shocking beyond words. It's awful! They think that their baby has been obligated by karma to come back and make up for his or her errors in previous lives. In other words, they think that God is some sort of sultan up in the skies punishing us because of our past transgressions. The fact is that we're all born without wisdom or understanding and can't help but make mistakes. We don't know any better and have to blunder to learn. Do you think God is going to condemn us for things beyond our control?

I asked a young father who believed that we reincarnate to atone for the sins of a past life if he'd punish his little boy without first telling him why he was being disciplined. He exclaimed, "No, of course not! I'd explain to my son what he'd done wrong."

I then said, "Well, you seem to have greater compassion than God, Who is boundless love, unlimited wisdom, and absolute harmony. By believing in karma, you're saying that the heavenly Father punishes His children even though they don't know what they've done wrong."

I think his belief is crazy. It insults my intelligence. I'm sure I couldn't convince a seven-year-old that God is so harsh and judgmental, because children are too smart to believe that kind of thing unless they've been brainwashed.

I've lectured in ashrams in India where Hindu traditions have kept the masses in subservience for centuries. For example, they've historically had a caste system in which one's role in society is determined at birth. The "untouchables" are people born to the lowest caste who are fated to suffer and be looked down upon all of their lives. Their rulers—those who have all the land, estates, and money—teach them that they must accept their poverty as karmic penalty for their past misdeeds and not try to change their situation. In a future incarnation, they're told, they'll be rewarded with a better life.

Isn't this just another way to hold people in bondage and keep them in misery? In my view, this belief system is an absolute lie and a living curse. No one is destined to live in poverty and spend a lifetime doing brutal labor. We're all here to rise, transcend, and grow. God is the Eternal Now and doesn't condemn people to suffer.

When you look at countries where the belief in predestination is prevalent, you find enormous misery, squalor, and filth. Yet the concept persists even in modern times. I've talked with guides in India who were well educated but said to me, "I'd better be careful and lead a better life or I may come back as a tiger or other animal."

⛨

Some years ago, I witnessed an experiment conducted on a friend of mine, a man we'll call "Mr. X." He was Roman Catholic and strongly disbelieved in reincarnation. However, a psychologist told him that he could hypnotize him and prove to him that he'd had many, many past lives. Their session would be recorded so that Mr. X could have evidence of their discussion when he came out of his trance.

Once Mr. X was hypnotized, the psychologist suggested to him that he'd now take him back 500 years and ask him to describe who he'd been in that life, where he'd lived, and what he'd done.

Mr. X didn't respond, so the psychologist continued, "Okay, now it's 1,000 years ago. Who are you? What's your name?" Again there was no reply from my friend.

Finally, the psychologist said in desperation, "I'm now regressing you to a time long, long ago—before England and Ireland were even heard of. Who were you in that life?"

There was silence for a minute, then Mr. X answered, "On the seventh day I rested."

This ended the hypnotic experiment on Mr. X. The reason for the failure is very simple: The subconscious mind always accepts the dominant of two ideas. In this instance, before he was hypnotized, Mr. X suggested to his subconscious, *I don't believe in reincarnation. I will give no response.* As a result, he neutralized the psychologist's suggestions and had no memories of a previous existence. Although it's generally true that people who've been put in a trance will cooperate and tell the hypnotist whatever he or she wants to hear—whether it's true or false—in this case, Mr. X's subconscious belief that reincarnation is false was stronger than the psychologist's suggestion.

Now, something very different happened when the psychologist hypnotized Mr. X's sister. She didn't fill her subconscious with a disbelief in reincarnation, and the doctor was able to regress her to a different period in history. While in a trance, she spoke French and claimed to be Joan of Arc. Then she was regressed to an even earlier era, and she described her life as a princess in Egypt and launched into an exposition on the religious beliefs of the region during ancient times. She also claimed that the pyramids were built by men who went into a trance and used the power of their minds to hew the enormous stones and set them in place.

There was, of course, no way of proving that she'd been Joan of Arc or an Egyptian princess. In talking with her, I learned that she'd studied French for four years and had lived in France. Furthermore, she'd also visited Egypt and had studied the history of the pyramids. In the trance state, her subconscious accepted the belief of the psychologist that she'd lived before and could talk about it. Her mind then used the knowledge at its command to act on the psychologist's suggestions. Her descriptions were a sort of composite of what she'd read and studied. This experiment provided further evidence that the subjective mind doesn't reason and will manifest any idea that we accept.

⇥✦⇤

Some people claim to remember previous incarnations and can even provide remarkable details about their past lives, including information about the era, location, and the interesting things that happened to them. They think that the only way they could have such memories is if they'd lived before, but that's actually not true. We're all immersed in the great pool of the universal mind. Our individual minds are connected to this reservoir that contains the experiences, reactions, and knowledge of everyone who's ever lived, including Jesus, Buddha, and Moses.

We have a memory of all languages and have been everywhere and seen everything because we're all part of Spirit. This is a simple spiritual truth. We're everyone who's ever lived, is living now, and will live in the future. There's nothing we don't know. If we go to India or Pakistan to see various temples, we might say, "I was here before . . . I remember this!" And we can find our way around the towns and cities as if we'd grown up there. This is a common experience because all lives and places are within us.

It's possible for you to be hypnotized, go back in time, and experience yourself as George Washington kneeling in the snow or Abraham Lincoln delivering the Gettysburg Address. However, this doesn't mean that you're a reincarnation of either of these men. You've simply tuned in to a mental picture or vibration that's forever embodied on the screen of the universal subjective mind. It's all registered in your own subconscious, which contains the sensory impressions of everyone who's ever lived. If you relax and think clearly, you'll perceive the One Intelligence Who wrote every great spiritual work and established all religions. This Divine Source within seeks to heal you.

In a Nutshell

In biblical times and still today, people wait for the messiah to come. But the messiah is *within* you. It's the God Presence that fills your mind and body. This Presence was never born and will never die, and It's instantly available to you right now.

By believing the theory of reincarnation, we fall from spiritual grace. Our subconscious belief that we must come back many times to atone for the sins and errors of our past lives keeps us in spiritual bondage and indicates that we have a guilt complex.

True reincarnation is the birth of God in your mind and heart. You can become intoxicated with the Divine right now and experience an ever-increasing measure of Spirit.

You can't be less tomorrow than you are today because life is growth, expansion, and newness. Life doesn't go backward or tarry with yesterday. It moves from glory to glory, strength to strength, and wisdom to wisdom. There's no end to our illumination.

Take time in the morning and evening to joyously affirm that the Infinite ocean of life, love, truth, and beauty is flowing through you, cleansing and healing your entire being. The wholeness and peace of God reign supreme in your mind and heart.

By teaching children who they really are—and by showing them the Way, the Truth, and the Light—we can build a heaven on Earth. We can stop the spread of undesirable states of consciousness that are perpetuated by prejudice, racial hatred, and fear of the unknown. We need to teach young people about the great accomplishments of artists, scientists, and mystics, for they tend to emulate what's presented to them.

Chapter Eight

Living an Inspired Life

*M*any people would experience a much more fulfilling life if only they had somebody to continually motivate and inspire them. They have no inclination to do this for themselves and consequently remain in mediocrity. They lack initiative and self-direction and have to be pushed about like the pieces on a checkerboard. After you give them a good talk and fire their ambition by telling them what's possible for them, they run splendidly for a few days, then suddenly collapse. All their power is gone, and they have to be recharged.

⌘

Many young people slide along the path of least resistance. They'd love to be successful but are afraid of the price. The obstacles seem insurmountable and require more perseverance than they want to muster. They have a vague idea that there's something good for them somewhere and that it will come along if they just wait long enough. In the meantime, they're content to be propped up and supported by others. This dependence on outside power and lack of self-reliance is fatal to all advancement. Those who can't stand on their own and who are always looking for help will never achieve an amazing life.

It's infinitely better to make mistakes than to never act on your own judgment. People who are always asking for advice and deferring to others never amount to much. They may be intelligent and well educated but lack the power of self-propulsion. They're invariably timid and hesitant followers who aren't needed anywhere. It's the independent leaders with backbone who are in demand. Whatever else these go-getters might lack, they never doubt themselves and inspire great confidence.

Nothing is more valuable than being able to give yourself an unqualified endorsement. It's the approval of that "still, small voice within" that says to every noble act, "That is right," and to every ignoble one, "That is wrong." If you resolve that you'll never do anything that provokes the least murmur from your conscience, you'll have a bulwark that will uphold you both in times of prosperity and in times of adversity and pain.

It matters very little what others may think about you or whether the press praises or blames you. Indeed, many people who are looked upon as successful, lauded in the daily papers, sought after by society, and admired by others know perfectly well that they're frauds. Every time they're complimented for their achievements, their conscience pricks them.

If you feel the least hint of disapproval from the still, small voice within, ask yourself what you're about to do and where it will lead. Something is wrong—of that you may be sure. And you must remedy it immediately. Don't parley with the cause of your disturbance, and don't try to compromise with it. That's as dangerous as a mariner in the midst of a storm insisting upon forcing his ship to sail in a particular direction. Trying to influence the compass will cause him to wreck his vessel on the rocks in his path. There are many, many human wrecks in the ocean of life who've ignored their own compass or tried to negotiate with it.

To keep your self-approval, you must be honest. No matter how slight your departure from truth or how trifling your deception (if any lie can be considered "minor"), you've tampered with the compass. If you persist in such a course, you won't reach the harbor you seek.

If you keep your self-approval, no matter what else you may lose you'll still be rich. You may make a fortune or forfeit one, live in a beautiful home or in an old boardinghouse, wear expensive clothes or cheap ones, ride in a fine automobile or walk, or have the good opinion of the world or its contempt . . . none of that matters if you've been honest, earnest, and true; believe in yourself; approve of your life; and can look yourself square in the face without wincing. Then you'll be successful even if the rest of the world brands you a failure.

You can't be mentally, morally, and physically healthy unless you persevere in fulfilling your ambitions. In striving to use your faculties to your full extent, you'll feel a contentment and satisfaction that can never come from just "getting by."

In a stirring address, President Theodore Roosevelt said, "In the last analysis a healthy state can exist only when the men and women who make it up lead clean, vigorous, healthy lives; when the children are so trained that they shall endeavor, not to shirk difficulties, but to overcome them; not to seek ease, but to know how to wrest triumph from toil and risk."

That's the secret of every successful and noble person who's ever lived. Perhaps life has been a bitter disappointment to you. In reviewing your past, you may feel that you've been a failure or at best have been plodding along in mediocrity. You may not have succeeded in the particular things you expected to, lost friends and relatives who were very dear to you, had your home wrenched from you because you couldn't pay the mortgage, or become so ill that you could no longer work. The new year may look discouraging to you. Yet in spite of any or all of these misfortunes, if you refuse to be conquered, victory is awaiting you farther down the road.

You're a pretty immature person if you lose the courage to face the world just because you've made a mistake or a slipup somewhere, your business has failed, your home has been swept away by some natural disaster, or because of some other trouble you were unable to avoid.

This is the test of your character: *How much is left in you after you've lost everything outside of yourself?* If you lie down now, throw up your hands, and give into defeat, there's not much in you. But if you refuse to give up, lose faith in yourself, or beat a retreat, you'll show that you're greater than your loss, stronger than your cross, and larger than any setback.

You may say that you've failed too often to get on your feet again and that there's no use in even trying. Nonsense! You haven't failed if your spirit is unconquered. No matter how late the hour or how many times you've been disappointed, success is still possible. We can look at hundreds of examples of men and women throughout history who have overcome losses, risen above the stupor of discouragement, and boldly faced forward once more.

If you haven't lost your courage, character, confidence, and self-respect, you're still a king. If you develop your grit and nerve, your misfortunes, losses, and disasters will make you stronger. As Henry Ward Beecher stated, "It is defeat that turns bone to flint; it is defeat that turns gristle to muscle; and it is defeat that makes men invincible."

Some people get along beautifully for half a lifetime, perhaps, as long as everything goes smoothly. While they're accumulating property and gaining friends and renown, their character seems to be strong and well balanced. But the moment trouble comes—a business failure, a bad investment, or other crisis—they're overwhelmed. They despair and lose the heart to try again. Their self-confidence is swallowed up by a mere material loss.

This is failure indeed, and there's little future for anyone who falls to such a depth of desperation. There's hope for an ignorant man who can't even write his name if he has stamina and backbone; for a cripple who has courage; and for a poverty-stricken woman who has nerve and grit. But there's no hope for those who cannot or will not stand up after they fall, lose heart when opposition strikes, and lay down their arms in defeat.

You can let everything else go if you have to, but never lose your grip on yourself. Don't relinquish your self-confidence. This is the priceless pearl, dearer to you than your breath. Protect it with all your might.

You should be so much greater than any material failure you suffer that the setback would scarcely be mentioned in your biography. It would be seen as a very minor incident in your career. The truly mature person possesses something that rises higher than worldly success or misfortune. No matter what reverses, disappointments, or calamities unfold, a great individual rises above them. In the midst of storms and trials to which a weaker nature would succumb, a strong person's serene soul and calm confidence assert themselves, so completely dominating all outward conditions that they have no power for harm.

⌖

There's something in our nature—a force that we can't describe or explain—that doesn't seem to reside in any of our ordinary faculties but lies much deeper in ourselves. It's a locked-up spiritual power that we don't normally call upon in our daily life; however, during extreme emergencies and supreme crises, it rushes to our assistance. It makes us giants and stamps us with the Divine seal.

If we use all the resources that God has planted within us, we can't fail. It would be strange indeed if the grandest of God's creatures were helpless and at the mercy of the accidents that make and ruin fortunes. Remember that there will be no failure if we realize our power and never let ourselves think that we're beaten.

⌖

So many times we face some obstacle that we think will be a terrible calamity and perhaps ruin us if we can't avoid it. We fear that our ambition will be thwarted or that our lives may be wrecked. Our dread of being overwhelmed is awful. Yet there are tens of thousands of examples of people who have triumphed over all sorts of handicaps and disheartening situations. Their stories negate all the excuses of those who today claim that they don't have a chance.

For example, Theodore Roosevelt, who was plagued by asthma and physical weakness as a child, took up the rough life of a ranch hand to build up his strength and went on to become a heroic soldier, hunter, naturalist, and, of course, leader of his country.

Also consider Simón Bolívar, who overcame personal tragedy to lead several South American countries in their struggle against Spain. Bolívar was born to a wealthy family in Venezuela in 1783 and was educated, like many of the young men of his class, in Spain. At age 19 he married a beautiful and accomplished daughter of a family of rank, and the couple embarked for America with the intention of caring for his estates. But shortly after they arrived, his wife died of yellow fever.

Her death changed his life. He resolved not to remarry and to instead devote himself to an important cause. Years later he said, "If it hadn't been for my wife's death, perhaps my life would have been different. I wouldn't have returned to Europe and had the ideas I gained from my travels, nor would I have made my study of the world, which has been of so much service to me during the course of my political career. Her death caused me to follow the chariot of Mars rather than the plow of Ceres."

After visiting many countries, he once again returned to Venezuela, where the first sparks of rebellion against Spain were kindling the revolution. He joined forces with the rebels and eventually became their leader. Over the next several years, Bolívar led the forces that liberated the regions that make up the modern countries of Venezuela, Colombia, Peru, Panama, Ecuador, and Bolivia. He's honored as a hero in those nations today and is known as "The Liberator."

If you're yearning to answer the call that runs in your blood but feel chained to overwhelming circumstances, it will take tremendous will and a powerful, iron constitution to overcome your challenges. If it's impossible to extricate yourself, the next best thing is to do what the oyster does with the grain of sand that it can't eject from its shell: Convert it into a pearl and make it as beautiful as possible. The constant exercising of grit and determination to make the best of an unfortunate situation is a dynamic force that builds character.

⊨✝⊨

One of America's great sculptors, Frederick Wellington Ruckstull, described how he overcame discouragement to pursue his dream:

> As a child in St. Louis, I was forever whittling but didn't have any thoughts about becoming a sculptor. When I was a little older, I thought I'd become a man of letters. I wrote for the newspapers and belonged to a prominent literary club. However, I drifted from one position to another and wondered if I'd ever succeed at anything. I went to Colorado; moved on to Arizona; and prospected, mined, and worked on a ranch. I went to California and at one time thought about shipping off to China. I returned to St. Louis and still wasn't sure what to do. I was becoming desperate.
>
> At that time, I went to an art exhibition and saw a clay sculpture. I said to myself, "I can do one as good as that," and I copied it. I told my friends that I was going to be a sculptor, but they laughed and teased me. I'd secured a position in a store and used my free time to do the art I'd always loved. Notices about me appeared in the newspapers as I became popular in the community. I entered a competition to win a commission to create a statue of General Frank R. Blair. I was selected, but when the committee discovered that I was only a clerk in a store, they argued that I wasn't competent to carry out the work, though they did give me the first-prize award of $150.
>
> Despite the recognition, my father and mother put every obstacle possible in my way. I wasn't even allowed to work on my sculptures in the attic.

I advanced at the store where I worked until I became assistant manager, earning $2,000 a year. When I told the proprietor that I'd decided to be a sculptor instead, he gazed at me in astonishment. "A sculptor?" he said incredulously, "Young man, why are you going to throw away the chance of a lifetime? I'll give you $5,000 a year and promote you to manager if you'll remain with me."

But I'd found my life's work. I knew that it would be a struggle and that I'd be poor until I attained fame, but I was confident in myself, which is half of the battle.

I saved up my money and went to Paris to study art but had to return to America to earn more so that I could continue my studies.

My family and friends laughed at me, and everyone discouraged me. But I secured seven orders to create busts for $200 each, to be completed after my return from France.

Ruckstull's refusal to be discouraged was rewarded. In the following years, he was commissioned to sculpt statues that can now be seen in museums, public buildings, parks, and private homes throughout the world.

According to a fable, one day a lion cub was playing alone in the wilderness while his mother slept. The baby lion decided that he'd explore a bit and see what the great world beyond his home was like. Before he realized it, he'd wandered so far that he couldn't find his way back. He was lost.

Very frightened, the cub ran frantically in every direction calling piteously for his mom, but she didn't hear him. Weary from searching, he didn't know what else to do. Then a sheep, whose offspring had been taken from her, heard his cries and adopted him.

The sheep became very fond of her foundling, who in a short while grew so large that at times she was almost afraid of him.

Often she'd detect a strange, far-off look in his eyes that she couldn't understand.

Nonetheless, the foster mother and her adopted cub lived very happily together until one day when a magnificent lion appeared, sharply outlined against the sky on the top of a nearby hill. He shook his tawny mane and uttered a terrific roar, which echoed through the countryside. The mother sheep stood paralyzed with fear, but the cub listened as though spellbound.

The lion's roar had touched a chord in his nature that he'd never felt before. New desires and a consciousness of his power possessed him. Instinctively he answered the lion's call with a corresponding roar.

Trembling with mingled fear, surprise, and bewilderment at the feelings aroused within him, the awakened animal gave his foster mother a last look and then, with a tremendous leap, started toward the lion on the hill.

The lost cub had found himself. Until then he'd gamboled around his sheep mother just as though he were a lamb, never dreaming that he could do anything different from the ordinary sheep around him. He hadn't imagined that he had within him a power that could strike terror in the other beasts of the jungle. Whereas he used to tremble at the mere howl of a wolf, he was now amazed to find that the animals that had terrified him before now fled from him.

As long as the baby lion thought he was a sheep, he was as timid and retiring as one. He had only a sheep's strength and courage and could never have exerted the command of a lion. If someone had suggested that he could, he would have asked, "How could I be so powerful? I'm only a sheep."

But when the lion was awakened in him, he instantly became a new creature, the king of beasts. The roar he heard hadn't given him any new abilities; it had merely brought forth what was already within him, revealing what he'd always possessed. Never again could this young animal be satisfied to act like a sheep. From then on he'd live as a lion.

There is in every human being a sleeping lion. It's just a question of rousing it . . . of finding something that will stir the depths of our being and awaken the powers within. Just like the cub, when we at last discover that we're more than mere clay and have the Divine Spirit within us, we shall never again be satisfied to live like a common clod of earth. We'll feel a new sense of strength welling up that we didn't know we possessed, and we'll no longer be content with low-flying ideals and cheap success. Instead, we'll seek higher and higher planes.

When you become conscious that the truth of your being is God and that you're inseparably connected to Spirit, you'll feel the thrill of Infinite force surging through every atom of your being and will never doubt the God Presence within or your potential. You'll no longer be timid, weak, hesitant, or fearful; and you'll know that your mission on Earth is Divinely planned and protected.

Many poor children grow up in the slums believing that they're like all the other kids in the neighborhood, with no special future ahead of them. But sometimes something unexpected happens— an emergency or some catastrophe that makes a tremendous call upon the greatness within themselves. They're surprised to discover that they're altogether different from those around them. They've seen that they have a tremendous latent power that they didn't know they possessed. They unhesitatingly answer the call and go out into the great world, never again satisfied with their former environment or beliefs.

There are men and women who have won distinction in their fields who wouldn't have believed that it was possible for them until they'd actually proved it. For example, when Charles M. Schwab was a young man, you could never have persuaded him that he'd rise from the position of laborer at Andrew Carnegie's steelworks to become president of the Carnegie Steel Company at age 35. He would have said, "Such a thing is absurd. I'm not a giant or a genius but am just an ordinary, hard-working man."

There are plenty of young people working at our many businesses and institutions today who couldn't be convinced that perhaps in a single year they'll be filling positions of great responsibility and power, yet the possibility is there. The future renowned general is today a soldier in the ranks; and tomorrow's successful executive is now an office clerk, messenger, or hamburger flipper.

It's the person you're capable of becoming, not who you are now, that's most important. You can't afford to carry this enormous asset to your grave unused. If you were a company president, you wouldn't think of leaving a lot of idle capital in a drawer, uninvested and earning no interest. Is this what you're doing with yourself?

You have assets within you that are infinitely more valuable than money. If you're not tapping into them, you're acting like an executive who's worried all the time about not being able to pay the bills when he or she has a large amount of capital getting dusty in the bank. It's even more irrational to leave Divine capital lying around unused. Why would you limp along in this little one-horse way all of your life when you have so much wealth in reserve?

Try to bring forth your enormous potential. You know that it's there and can instinctively feel it. Your intuition and ambition tell you that there's much more in you than you've ever discovered or used. Why don't you stir it up and call it out? Once you've uncovered a bit of your Divine pattern, you'll never be content until you bring the rest of your true nature to light.

The world has a right to expect those who've become even partially conscious of their Divine origins to do their work a little better, live on a higher plane, and set a helpful example for those who haven't yet experienced their hidden power. The planet needs these great inspirations more than it needs fantastic engineers, lawyers, physicians, ministers, or politicians. Our souls are hungrier for a Lincoln than for more brilliant magnates, financiers, or inventors.

After listening to a beautiful concert or going to an opera, people may feel the release of something inside them—something that they never really knew they possessed until then. For instance, take the case of a young woman who has wonderful musical abilities slumbering in her depths but who has always lived on a farm in the country. She's never come in contact with musical or artistic people and has never heard music of any account outside her little church choir. She remains quite ignorant of her latent possibilities until she goes to the city and hears famous musicians and singers. Then a new passion is aroused in her, and her career plans are instantly changed. She has discovered a force in herself that will henceforth govern her life.

Sometimes a great play will have a similar effect upon people. They leave the theater feeling conscious that dormant forces within them have been awakened. It's important to seek out every possible experience that promises to reveal your nature and release your possibilities.

⚜

One of the great advantages of education and wide experience is that they help us to uncover more and more of our hidden powers. These inner capabilities are inexhaustible, for no matter how many discoveries we make about ourselves, there's no diminution of our potential. In fact, human life seems to be like a funnel: We pass into the small end at birth, and the further we go, the wider the funnel opens. Our horizon keeps pushing toward the Infinite, and there appears to be no limits to our possible growth.

Unfortunately, many people go through life without uncovering their true nature to any great extent because they don't seek opportunities for growth. They don't take sufficient pains to put themselves in an environment that sparks their ambitions or try to surround themselves with individuals who will inspire them to expand their lives. On the other hand, men and women who try to make the most of themselves never stop growing. They're always progressing on the road because they continually set new goals for themselves as they flourish and prosper. They only stop briefly at way stations to drop off a few things they no longer need—impediments that hamper them—and then resume their journey.

If you want to find your own buried resources and stimulate your growth, you must strive to improve yourself in various ways and broaden your mental and spiritual outlook. You can increase your intelligence through keener observation and the continual study of people and things. You can also develop yourself by enlarging the sphere of your service to others. Finally, I know of no means of self-discovery so potent as an inspiring book. It's a wonderful idea to keep uplifting works near you so that you can refer to them often.

We become great to the extent that we learn to know ourselves and develop our faculties. The more deeply we draw upon our resources, the more of our hidden self we discover and the wider our vision grows.

Listening to a great speaker often stirs us to the very center of our being and awakens desires, powers, and determination that have been asleep. Perhaps you experienced this when you heard a great minister or lecturer who seemed to open up a realm in your soul that might otherwise have remained forever hidden.

Think of the secret chambers of possibility that have been unlocked in a multitude of people by great leaders such as Abraham Lincoln. There are thousands of individuals living today who are grander men and women, better husbands and wives, and stronger doctors and political leaders because of Lincoln's example.

It will make all the difference in the world if you surround yourself with people who believe in you and encourage the development of your abilities. If you interview the great army of failures, you'll find that many have been defeated because they never put themselves in a stimulating environment that would ignite their ambition or they weren't strong enough to rally themselves in the face of depressing or vicious surroundings. Most of the people we find in prisons and on welfare are pitiable examples of the negative influence of an environment that appealed to the worst in them instead of to the best.

Whatever else you may do in life, make any sacrifice necessary to stay in a positive environment that will motivate you to greater self-development. Keep close to the people who understand you, believe in you, and will encourage you to make the most of yourself. This may make all the difference between your having a grand success and leading a mediocre existence.

Spend your time with people who are trying to do something and to be somebody in the world—those with high aims and sincere intentions. Determination is contagious, and you'll catch the spirit that dominates your environment. The success of those around you who are trying to climb high will encourage you to keep going if you haven't done quite so well yourself. Their strength and achievement act as a great magnetic force that will help you attract the object of your ambition. It's incredibly stimulating to be with people whose aspirations run parallel with your own. If you lack energy, are naturally lazy, or are inclined to take it easy, you'll be urged forward by the constant prodding of the more ambitious.

In a Nutshell

It's infinitely better to make mistakes than to never act on your own judgment. People who always ask for advice and defer to others rarely amount to much even if they have a lot of talent and education. They lack the power of self-propulsion and are invariably followers rather than leaders. They're not in much demand because it's the qualities of independence, self-reliance, and backbone that are most valued.

To keep your own self-approval, you must be honest. No matter how slight your departure from truth or how trifling your deception (if any lie can be considered "minor"), you're tampering with your internal compass. If you persist in such a course, you won't reach the harbor you seek.

Let go of everything else if you must but never lose your own esteem. This is a priceless pearl and is dearer to you than your breath. Protect it with all your might.

Perhaps the past has been a bitter disappointment for you. In reviewing it, you may feel that you've been a failure or at best have been plodding along in mediocrity. Yet in spite of any setbacks, if you refuse to be conquered, victory is awaiting you farther down the road.

Try to bring forth your enormous potential. You know that it's there and can instinctively feel it. Your intuition and ambition tell you that there's much more in you than you've ever discovered or used. Why don't you stir it up and call it out?

$$\textit{Chapter Nine}$$

Getting Results from Prayer

A happy, successful life must flow from a well-balanced mind that has a sense of absolute security and faith in the Creator. We must be rooted in the Eternal truths and know that we're part of the Infinite Mind that manifests and governs all things. We experience true peace when we know that nothing can wrench us out of our orbit and that no accident, disease, or discord can separate us from our union with the One Power. When we know that nothing can cheat us out of our birthright and that every right step must lead to ultimate triumph, we can serenely accomplish the highest good that lies in our power.

Having a deep sense of uncertainty, on the other hand, is fatal to happiness. No matter what religious tradition we practice, the belief that a Higher Power created us and always guides us is essential. In short, without faith in God, there's no way we can achieve a fulfilling life.

For an untold number of centuries, people prayed to the forces and influences of nature, which were distant and removed from their lives. These were their gods. Gradually their attempts to appease the deities became formalized and ritualized and were usually offered through an intermediary: a priest or tribal leader who was considered to possess superior knowledge or have a special relationship with the gods or God. Such practices are still prevalent, but over many years, there has been a growing emphasis upon religion as an *individual* relationship with the Eternal truths.

The long transition from mediated prayer to prayer as a personal mystical experience has been the work of dedicated enlightened seers—the teachers of wisdom. They've known that the primary purpose of prayer is to remember our oneness with God and become all that we're intended to be. As our awareness and recognition increase, it becomes possible to realize our unity with the Healing Presence and experience "at-one-ment." We feel the love, strength, and purpose that goes beyond our understanding, for the Infinite Being is a mystery.

Achieving serenity of spirit and peace of mind is one of the most advanced lessons of cultures everywhere, and it flows from a perfect trust in the all-powerful Omnipresence.

In the Bible we read that the disciples observed Jesus praying. When he'd finished, one of them said, "Lord, teach us to pray." The unnamed disciple uttered the aspiration that everyone holds, for true prayer is the realization of one's desires through the action of the law of God Who rules over everything.

Jesus taught them the following prayer:

> *Our Father in heaven,*
> *Hallowed be your name.*
> *Your kingdom come.*
> *Your will be done,*
> *   on earth as it is in heaven.*

Give us today our daily bread,
and forgive us our debts,
*   as we also have forgiven our debtors.*
And lead us not into temptation,
*   but deliver us from evil.*
For yours is the kingdom and the power and the glory, forever.

Most men and women brought up and educated in the Christian tradition probably memorized this great passage, popularly known as "The Lord's Prayer," very early in life. It's regularly recited during worship services and has inspired millions of the Christian faith. However, it's also a truly universal prayer that can help people of all religious beliefs on this planet in this moment. Jesus gave us a practical metaphysical formula that lays out the definite steps that anyone can use to achieve a more rewarding and fulfilling life.

The first step is recognizing that we require more than intellect alone to supply our needs. As wonderful and knowledgeable as our mind may be, it creates nothing because it's "the Father within Who doeth the works." We therefore direct our attention to our Father in heaven, Who isn't a person but is Divine Intelligence. Once we recognize that everything is part of this One Infinite Mind, we discover heaven, the rarified state of creative power.

In the second step, we acknowledge our union with the Higher Power and experience the peace of God filling our mind and heart. This is the meaning of the phrase "Your kingdom come." The experience can't be described in mere words but can only be felt within. We remove our attention from the evidence of our five senses and feel the spontaneous upliftment of the Divine.

In this powerful state of oneness with God, we enter the third step, which is the adoration and realization that there is a Higher Presence and Power that cares for us and is eager to heal us and fulfill our needs. The "daily bread" mentioned in the prayer represents far more than physical sustenance; it's also the bread that nourishes our soul. We need to partake of goodness, courage, beauty, joy, peace, and all the other inspiring qualities. The Infinite Mind is there for us, waiting to come forth and provide anything we can conceive. Our "debts," the old habits that no longer serve us, are forgiven as we establish new, life-giving patterns in our mind.

The fourth step is thanksgiving. We praise God, knowing that our prayer has already been answered. The Bible states that our heavenly Father knows what we need before we even ask. We offer our gratitude that we're whole, perfect, and complete.

The Lord's Prayer is the prayer of a king, not the petition of a beggar. It's an affirmation of Divine consciousness and is as magnificent and pertinent today as it was when Jesus taught it more than 2,000 years ago.

There's something in our very consciousness that tells us that we're not mere products of chance and that fear and doubt are unnecessary. We have an inner sense that we're inseparable from the One Mind and were created in the image of God. Therefore, our ultimate purpose can't conflict with the Divine's ultimate purpose. We instinctively know that there must be a unity to all things and that the best way to find it is to trust God. Once we feel the thrill of the Infinite pulse that comes from the heart of truth and being, we shall no longer doubt, hesitate, or be satisfied with the superficial and the temporary. Once the soul tastes its rightful food, it's no longer content to grovel for scraps.

When we awaken in the morning, refreshed and rejuvenated, we know that we've been in touch with the Divine that created us and are made anew.

Our mind is a tool, a pen with which we write our book of life. If we don't like what we've inscribed, we have the authority to write some more and change the story. Our experience assumes the form, shape, and quality of our words, thoughts, and feelings. It's a perfect reflection of our consciousness. The minute we state, "I'm troubled," the formless Presence responds by coming forth and manifesting as negative events. Likewise, the instant we say, "I know that there's a solution," the Infinite begins to present a wonderful answer—something greater than we could imagine.

Our prayers are answered not because we repeat specific words or follow rituals but because we put great feeling and awareness into our affirmations. Our emotions enable us to contact the Father within, Who is intelligent and creative does everything necessary to manifest our desires. As the poet James Montgomery wrote: "Prayer is the soul's sincere desire, Uttered or unexpressed—the motion of a hidden fire That trembles in the breast."

When we're weary and sad, how we long to feel our union with our Divine Presence and quench our thirst at the great Fountain-head. We can go within to our inner sanctuary, where we meet and talk with God. We need to remove our attention from our problems, because as long as our mind is centered on negativity, there will be no change for the better.

We can't see the Spirit of God but we can feel It as we go into our secret place and shift our focus from the evidence our physical senses and the outer world. We enter the realm of pure feeling, the arena of undifferentiated Mind and formless Being. In this consciousness, we feel the enthusiasm and animation of God and assume the mood of knowing that our prayer is already answered. Infinite Mind is a perfect, creative agent; and whatever we focus our thoughts on will be demonstrated.

❧✝❧

We'll never reach our highest potential until we learn that the Life Principle is as indestructible as the laws of mathematics. Even if all the math books in the world were destroyed by fire, two plus two would still equal four. The principles of math wouldn't be affected in the least by the demise of the texts. In the same way, we can maintain our equanimity in the face of any disaster. God hasn't made a mistake, and His highest creation—human beings—aren't placed at the mercy of random accidents.

The moment we realize that we're part of a great Power and are made to dominate rather than be dominated, we'll rise to meet every situation in a masterly, serene way instead of in a cringing manner.

When we come to a full realization of our Divinity, we won't be thrown off course or disturbed by the vexing events that trouble those who haven't yet learned the secret of prayer. We'll realize the desires of our heart by calling upon the Presence and Power of God within us.

❧✝❧

What is it that prompts us to pray? Usually it's something in our personal world that we want to change or improve. However, the purpose of prayer isn't to alter people, things, or conditions or to beg for some kind of help. Instead, the goal is to achieve a change and improvement in our *consciousness* . . . to rise to a higher dimension or go to another "mansion in our Father's house." We pray to lift our consciousness and to bring something *into*—rather than out of—existence.

In counseling with men and women, I'm often asked, "How could I possibly not be full of fear? I have a terrible and perplexing problem, and I'll lose my home if I can't pay my mortgage by next Friday."

This is why the Bible bids us to go into our inner sanctuary and remove our attention from our worldly problems: "When you pray, go into your room, and when you have shut your door, pray to your Father who is in the secret *place;* and your Father who sees in secret will reward you openly."

Prayer causes a psychological and emotional transformation. We go from feeling fear, lack, and despair to experiencing courage, confidence, and joy. It's a metaphysical truth that every change in our circumstances and conditions must be preceded by a change in consciousness. *According to our beliefs, it is done unto us.*

In the Bible it says that the "son of man" is given all power and glory. On a symbolic level, the *son* represents each of us. We're all heirs to the inner kingdom. We therefore must assume our sovereignty— that is, we need to control and direct our faculties and focus on the Power and Presence within even though we can't see It. We *can* feel the Infinite Divine, and our convictions will manifest. Our desires are assuming shape, form, and substance now. *Ours is the kingdom and the glory.*

Whenever we're tempted to revert to old patterns of fear, doubt, and impatience, it's the *habit* that has tempted us, not God. Viewing God as a foe is an erroneous idea in the mind, for He doesn't try to lead us astray.

When we realize that we're Divine Eternal Principle, nothing can throw us off balance. We'll be centered in the everlasting truth and free from the taint of all worry, blame, and despair.

Everyone has experienced personal slights, hurt, and dishonesty. These psychic wounds can and must be forgiven, because if we mentally feast on anger, spite, and mistreatment, we're guaranteeing that we'll experience pain and betrayal again and again. We need to forgive ourselves and everyone else to establish an entirely new, life-giving pattern.

The majority of people are acting and reacting from their own wounds and are ignorant of the mental and spiritual laws. They're therefore emotionally impaired; and we shouldn't be resentful, angry, or impatient toward them. After all, we're usually moved to compassion when we meet someone who's physically handicapped. We can offer this same love to those who suffer from emotional illness. It's actually in our own self-interest to give up feeling mad and bitter because God can only grant us that which we're aware of and focus on. It's wiser to choose peace and goodwill. *The kingdom, the power, and the glory are yours now and forever.*

In a Nutshell

A sense of uncertainty or doubt is fatal to a happy life. We must be rooted in the truth of being and feel an unwavering faith that we're part of the Infinite Intelligence that creates and governs all things.

The purpose of prayer is to help us to remember and become all that we're intended to be. Prayer assists us in expanding our minds and achieving a transformation of consciousness that will bring all good into our lives. It's a metaphysical truth that every change in our circumstances and environment must be preceded by a change in our awareness.

You can use prayer to realize the desires of your heart through the Divine Presence and Power within. Go into the inner sanctuary of God and remove your attention from the evidence of the five senses and the outer world. Enter the realm of pure feeling and affirm: "God knows me and cares about me and is now creating and bringing forth a solution that is far superior to anything I could possibly come up with." You'll feel a sense of peace fill your mind and heart.

Everyone has experienced personal slights, hurt, and dishonesty. These psychic wounds can and must be forgiven, because if we mentally feast on anger, spite, and mistreatment, we're guaranteeing that we'll experience pain and betrayal again and again. We need to forgive ourselves and everyone else to establish an entirely new, life-giving pattern.

Chapter Ten

How to Think with Authority

You become what you think about all day long. When you dwell on a thought, you're actually releasing its latent power into action. This is why the Bible tells us: "Whatever things are true, whatever things are noble, whatever things are just, whatever things are pure, whatever things are lovely, whatever things are of good report, if there is any virtue and if there is anything praiseworthy—meditate on these things."

This passage can serve as a spiritual yardstick. If you read anything in a book or newspaper, or you hear a lecture or anything at all that isn't noble and praiseworthy, it's false and should be rejected. When you think along these lines, you're truly acting from the standpoint of the Eternal verities that never change.

Have a healthy respect for your thoughts, because your well-being, happiness, success, and peace of mind are largely determined by your awareness of the mind's power. When you definitively know that your thoughts are a force in their own right, you'll be able to pray effectively. After all, the oak is already latent in the acorn. You can't give the seed vitality and form because it already has its own mechanics and mode of expression. In the same way, you can't give power to your thoughts because they already contain the blueprint and energy to manifest. When you know this, you're freed from strain and anxiety.

Most people don't understand what thought really is. What they call "thinking" is actually just reacting to the environment. They read a newspaper or hear a commentator and begin to think along those lines. In fact, the majority of individuals don't use their own mind but adopt the ideas of a politician, a columnist, a friend, or a grandmother. This isn't genuine thought, which only occurs when we wrestle with opposing concepts, reason our way to a Divine conclusion, and say, "This is the truth." We fish the answer from the deeper mind.

Realize that the Infinite Intelligence within knows the answer to any problem under the sun. When you call upon It, It answers you, for Its nature is responsiveness. Know that your subconscious always responds and that you'll recognize its message as it flashes into your mind.

If you believe that you're going to fail, you're not really thinking, because there's no principle of defeat. The Infinite Being is *always* successful, whether It makes a star, a sun, a moon, or a tree. Therefore, even though you may stumble three or four times in some undertaking, you haven't failed. These attempts are just stepping-stones toward your triumph. When you believe in the principle of success, the Almighty Power backs you up and compels you toward victory. That's true thinking, because you're acting from the perspective of Divine Intelligence.

If you want to get results in your life, recognize the supremacy of Spirit and the authority of your thought. Sometimes the answers will come to you in a dream or vision. For example, Einstein's concept of the universe came to him in a flash when he was sound asleep. Similarly, sometimes good detectives will study a case and meditate upon it. They affirm that their subconscious has complete knowledge of who perpetrated the crime, where they live, and their habits. These detectives still their conscious mind and call upon the subconscious to provide an answer. Before falling asleep at night, they dwell upon the solution. Sometimes the answer is revealed in a dream, and sometimes when they wake up in the morning or are eating breakfast, the solution pops into their head. Then they know the exact spot to find the criminals and can apprehend them.

When the media reports that a disease is spreading, some people panic because fear is contagious. A discussion of earthquakes or other disasters may frighten us too if we fall victim to every wind that blows through our mind. We react with anxiety because we don't know who we are or where we're going. We don't know how to think. If there's any doubt, worry, or trepidation in our thoughts, we're not actually thinking. Instead, the mass or race mind is thinking through us and making a mess of our lives. Fear is faith in the wrong things, ignorance of the nature of Divine Spirit, and a conglomeration of shadows in the mind.

The truth is that there's no principle of fear; there's only a principle of love. We only feel afraid when we have a false conception of God, Who in reality is joy, beauty, life, truth, and glory. And what's true of God is always true of each of us.

Do you know the way many people think? They revert to their childhood acceptance of their fathers' beliefs. Perhaps your own dad was dogmatic and tyrannical when you were young. Maybe he told you, "You have to go to church every Sunday, and every night you must kneel down and say your prayers."

Now you hate all religions and say, "They're all a racket." You're trying to get even with your father but you don't know why and you don't know what you're doing. You're acting unconsciously. You may believe that you're thinking for yourself, but you're not.

You should learn to use your own mind rather than either blindly rejecting or adopting what you learned as a child. Perhaps everything your parents taught you about religion was their misinterpretation of the true meaning of the Bible.

Are you saying, "Mother wouldn't like it if I joined a church of Religious Science"? You don't have to try to win her approval or reject her. She may think differently from you, but of course you can still love her. You can say, "Mom, I don't think that way anymore. I have a new vision and conception of life." Then you bless her and let her believe whatever she wants, too.

Believe in the goodness and love of God. He doesn't tell you to hate your father or mother—He only says to turn away from their false beliefs. To *hate* someone is to be vindictive and full of anger and to murder love, peace, joy, and beauty. Harboring such negative feelings may give you cancer, tuberculosis, arthritis, or some other disease. Your beliefs reach a point of saturation within you and precipitate a great tragedy in your life. You might ask, "Why did this happen to me?" Well, it's because you're committing murder in your heart every morning, noon, and night.

☩

The Bible says: "You shall love the Lord your God with all your heart, all your soul, and all your strength." God is the Living Spirit within you . . . the Supreme Cause, Presence, and Substance. He is

Infinite. There couldn't be two Powers because one would cancel out the other and chaos would erupt everywhere. Indeed, science tells us that infinity has no beginning or end and that we can't multiply or divide it. There is therefore only One Power moving as unity.

Love in the Bible means "to honor" and realize that God is Omnipotent and All-Knowing. We need to devote ourselves to this Being and give no power to the sun, moon, stars, neighbors, trees, or rocks. We don't say that the night air will make us sick or that malevolent entities are lurking among us.

If you want peace of mind, avoid the poison of resentment; and if you want love in your heart, reject ill will. Don't hate anyone but wish for everyone all the blessings of heaven. When you're in trouble or facing sickness or anything of that nature, don't fight the problem. Turn your attention away from it and realize that the Savior is within you. The Bible says: "My spirit rejoices in God, my Savior . . . " Surely you don't worship two gods! There's only One Infinite Intelligence. It made your body and knows how to heal you. You need to turn with confidence to the Divine and claim that It guides you. Mentally abandon your negative state and contemplate the solution. Persevere and you shall be "saved," which means receiving the answer to your problem.

In the 18th century, Franz Mesmer healed people by placing his hands on their body. He called it "magnetizing" and believed that a magnetic fluid emanated from him into others, thereby restoring their health. He didn't know why it worked but brought about marvelous cures for many people.

Freud later explained that Mesmer's method was effective because of the power of the unconscious or subconscious mind. When Mesmer told his patients that the touch of his hands could heal them, the power of his suggestion influenced their subconscious and brought about a cure.

Some theologians have taught that morality is based upon what you do with your body. If you don't drink alcohol, smoke, dance, or eat the wrong foods, you're virtuous. Some ministers have preached that playing cards is sinful, that women should wear dresses down to their toes, and that movies and other kinds of entertainment are immoral.

Such beliefs are ignorant. As a result of these many injunctions, women become frigid, men feel frustrated and inhibited, and some become psychiatric cases.

In fact, you're more than just your body—you're a temple of the Living God. You're here to transform your thoughts. When you do so, you change your destiny. To *repent* doesn't mean that you need to wear sackcloth and put ashes on your face; it means that you begin to think from the standpoint of the Eternal verities. You focus on what's true, lovely, noble, and godlike. Then and only then are you truly thinking.

You're not just a body but a mental and emotional being. You don't live in your physical self but in your mind. You can think, feel, see, and travel independent of your body. You can leave it right now!

Your consciousness makes your body every second of the day. Your thoughts become tissue, muscle, and bone. Thousands of old cells are continually dying and new ones are being born. If your thoughts are positive, the Healing Power flows through you and makes you whole and perfect.

Remember that whatever you impress on your subconscious is expressed in the outer world. It's wonderful to fill your mind with love, peace, and joy because you're then compelled to express these qualities. Also, if you meditate on whatever is beautiful and true as often as possible, you'll be moved to love your spouse and children and speak kindly to them. Why? Because you become what you dwell upon all day long.

If you decide on something in your mind, your body always carries out your command. The process never errs because the subconscious is the major operator of your life. You're like an iceberg: 90 percent of you is subconscious, while only 10 percent of you exists above the ocean. When you walk, swim, type, or catch a ball, you're doing it automatically, through the power of the subconscious. These patterns have been conveyed to your deeper mind through repetition. In the same way, when you regularly and systematically convey beneficial ideas to your subconscious, it becomes a habit.

If you fail to make a conscious decision, you're saying, "I won't decide and will take whatever comes." Then you're operating from the race or mass mind that believes in misfortune, sickness, tragedy, death, fires, explosions, and hardship. Although this global mind contains some good, most of what it professes is negative. The race consciousness impinges on your own mind, reaches a point of saturation, and precipitates as disaster in your life.

If you don't focus on the Divine Spirit, the fears, doubts, aches, and jealousies of the mass mind will invade you like mice and insects infest a house that's not kept clean. What happens to the home that is your mind when you don't meditate and pray? Do you think that you're going to have happiness, peace, and abundance and that everything is going to be lovely? You won't! Eternal vigilance is the price of liberty. You need to continually fill your mind with the truths of God in order to counteract the false ideas of the world.

You can say, "I'm a Catholic [or a Protestant, Jew, Christian Scientist, Muslim, or whatever]," but your words are absolutely meaningless if you don't practice the Presence of God in your own heart. The only thing that matters is what you truly believe with all your soul. You can write a beautiful dissertation on Divine laws of mind but be full of hatred, jealousy, or bigotry. In fact, the religion of millions of people is fear. But if you give your allegiance to God, you'll bring forth health, happiness, peace, and all the blessings of life. *As a man thinketh in his heart, so is he.*

You can change your subconscious mind by feeding it with life-giving patterns. This is called *prayer* or the harmonious interaction of your subconscious and conscious mind. When these two work in harmony, you experience joy and abundance. But when they operate in discord, you get disease, death, misfortune, war, crime, and every other negative thing in the universe.

Unless you spiritually activate your mind, you're just allowing the debris of the race mind to pollute your subconscious. For example, when a husband and wife are continually fighting, look at what happens to their home and bank account. Their lives are most likely a mess. Or consider the nature of war: Horrific conflicts are simply an aggregation of individuals whose minds are at war.

Since there's only *One* Power, separate forces of "good" and "evil" don't exist. If you use the Power within you constructively and harmoniously, people call It *God, Allah,* or *Brahma;* and if you use It destructively, they say It's *Satan, the adversary, evil,* and so on. In fact, whether something is good or bad depends upon what you do with it. For instance, you can use electricity to kill somebody or cook your dinner, but the energy is still part of the One Divine Intelligence.

When you're engrossed in something, you're thinking with authority and are creating your destiny. The subconscious mind produces the equivalent of the idea that you impress upon it. Prayer is therefore not a nebulous thing but the deliberate, conscious selection of a spiritual thought, plan, or purpose. You nourish an idea and envelop it in love and expectancy—and what you expect, you create. Your desires will automatically come to pass.

Many people are uncomfortable with this teaching because they want to pray to an old man in heaven surrounded by saints and angels dancing around a throne. All of this, of course, is childish and immature. There's no gold throne up in the sky. God is *within* you. He is Spirit and is formless and unbounded. He's not more active or present in my life than in yours, for the Indivisible One is everywhere at all times. Divine Intelligence knows what to do and how to do it.

If you say, "I have free will," but then complain, "I can't give up drinking or smoking," "I can't lose weight," or "I can't make ends meet," you're denying the Presence and Power of God within you. In this instance, you're an atheist because you're declaring, "God can't heal me."

Stop being a nonbeliever ! Don't deny the Power of God within you. If you say, "I'm stymied and stuck," you're thinking from the standpoint of the race mind or the law of averages. You're claiming that God doesn't know the way out and isn't all-wise. You're saying that you can't change your circumstances, but of course you can. You just don't want to.

"I can't get well," you might lament. Who said so? You did! You're the only thinker in your mind, and that's why you're not healing. You can go for help to all the doctors and metaphysicians in town, but if you believe your case is hopeless, it will be. Start by saying, "I can get well. It's possible for me to be healed, because with God all things are possible." Make up your mind. If you can decree a thing, it shall come to pass. You may just be too lazy to do it—that's all. You *can* do it if you think from the perspective of possibility. Say yes! to life. Chant the beauty of the good and stop whining about the bad. Only then are you thinking with authority.

When you focus on an idea, your subconscious will execute it. Your conscious mind and subconscious—your brain and heart—act in concert to bring forth your invention. It's possible to manifest all the money and love you want because God is the greatest force in the universe—more powerful than dynamite, earthquakes, nuclear weapons, or anything else you can think of.

Some people agree that God is all-powerful, yet lead defeated lives and feel frustrated, neurotic, and unhappy. The hospitals are full of sick individuals who say that they believe in the Bible, the Koran, or other religious teachings. The problem is that their belief is purely intellectual. It's not a living truth in their heart. They talk about God and the law and can get a 100 percent on their metaphysics exam, but they're the most neurotic people in town because they haven't filled themselves with their faith.

You see, you must demonstrate what you believe in, because a faith without works is dead. Your belief must be evidenced in your mind, body, pocketbook, and relationships. Is there a light in your eyes? Are you dancing to the rhythm of God? Are you illumined and inspired? Are you full of the bliss of God? How often do you laugh at yourself? If you don't do so six or seven times a day, then you're not really spiritual. Don't worry though, for you *can* learn to become spiritual—to grow, expand, and unfold.

Stop saying, "I'm seeking God." How can you seek Him when He's already within you? When you discover the law of mind, you've found God. The Bible says: "In the beginning was the Word, and the Word was with God, and the Word was God."

Stop talking about the law or the word of God and use it. Many people have endless discussions about the Divine but fail to go deep enough to let It dominate them. If you say, "God is peace" and let thoughts of peace dominate your mind, you'll feel calm and relaxed. Furthermore, you'll have joy instead of gloom and suffer no lack in your life. You won't be sick because you believe that God is whole and perfect. Since God is your reality, you're also healthy and complete. If you believe in the goodness, joy, love, and harmony of the Infinite, you'll lead a charmed life.

Everything you see in the world, including the cities, buildings, cars, and airplanes, came from the One Mind. And this Mind is the mind of humankind, for there is only One Source. All inventions and wealth begin as an idea in the Infinite Intelligence that flows through you at all times. You're an inlet and an outlet to all that is. You must think about what you want and *feel* its reality. Get excited about your desire and let your enthusiasm for it fill your heart. Then your thought becomes electrified and manifests in your outer world.

On the other hand, if you wish to have better health but believe that some germ has the power of infection or that cancer can metastasize all over your body, you won't be healed. You're not thinking with authority but from the perspective of ignorance. The truth is that God made you and is all-powerful. There's no principle of disease—it's simply an error or false direction in your mind, and sickness can't be sustained if you don't feed your subconscious negative thoughts about illness.

The Healing Power is within you and the tendency of Life is toward perfect wholeness and wellness.

Change your belief and you'll think with authority. You'll have a strong conviction in your heart about the supremacy of Spirit and will know that disease and all other external things are powerless.

⇥✠⇤

Where is the mind? Some people say it's in the brain, but you know very well that it's not there. If you put a brain on a shelf, does it think? You can feel, smell, move, and think independent of both your brain and your body. You can move objects, travel thousands of miles, and report what you see without using your physical self.

The elusive thing that some people call "mind" or "thought" is real and lies hidden in the midst of matter. Behind the brain is the thinker, and behind the universe is a thought. This isn't a new idea—it was written in the Upanishad thousands of years ago that "God thinks, and worlds appear." And that Thinker is in each one of us. You're the only Cause in your universe and are responsible for your thoughts. Your spouse, boss, and neighbors aren't in charge of your thinking; nor is anybody else. We all live, move, and have our being in God; and He lives, moves, and has His being in us.

Realize that your eyes are God's eyes and that you're seeing the glory, the beauty, and the depth of the Eternal One. He is a lamp unto your feet and a light upon your path. As you control your mind and govern your thoughts, you'll bring forth a thousand joys. God's river of peace floods your mind, your heart, and your entire being.

In a Nutshell

Most people don't understand what thought is. What they call "thinking" is actually just reacting to the environment. They don't have their own thoughts but borrow the ideas of politicians, columnists, or relatives. They read an editorial and blindly adopt its opinion. True thinking is when we wrestle with opposing ideas, reason our way to a Divine conclusion, and say, "This is the truth."

If you want peace of mind, avoid resentment; and if you want love in your heart, reject ill will. Don't hold grudges against anyone but wish for everyone to have all the blessings of heaven.

Remember that whatever you impress on your subconscious is expressed in your outer world. It's wonderful to fill your deeper mind with thoughts of love, peace, and joy, because then you're compelled to experience and embody these qualities.

If you continually meditate on whatever is lovely, true, noble, and godlike, you'll be compelled to love your spouse and children and speak kindly to them. Why? Because you become what you think about all day long.

You can say, "I'm a Catholic [or a Protestant, Jew, Muslim, Christian Scientist, or whatever]," but your words have absolutely no meaning if you don't practice the Presence of God in your own heart. The only thing that matters is what you deeply believe in your soul.

Prayer is the interaction of your subconscious and conscious mind. When these two work together in unison and harmony, you experience health, happiness, and peace. But when they operate in discord, you get disease, death, misfortune, war, and crime.

You're the only thinker in your world and are responsible for your thoughts. Your spouse, boss, and neighbors aren't in charge of your thinking; nor is anybody else. We all live, move, and have our being in God; and He lives, moves, and has His being in us.

Biography of Joseph Murphy

*J*oseph Murphy was born on May 20, 1898, in a small town in the County of Cork, Ireland. His father, Denis Murphy, was a deacon and professor at the National School of Ireland, a Jesuit facility. His mother, Ellen, née Connelly, was a housewife, who later gave birth to another son, John, and a daughter, Catherine.

Joseph was brought up in a strict Catholic household. His father was quite devout and, indeed, was one of the few lay professors who taught Jesuit seminarians. He had a broad knowledge of many subjects and developed in his son the desire to study and learn.

Ireland at that time was suffering from one of its many economic depressions, and many families were starving. Although Denis Murphy was steadily employed, his income was barely enough to sustain the family.

Young Joseph was enrolled in the National School and was a brilliant student. He was encouraged to study for the priesthood and was accepted as a Jesuit seminarian. However, by the time he reached his late teen years, he began to question the Catholic orthodoxy of the Jesuits, and he withdrew from the seminary. Since his goal was to explore new ideas and gain new experiences—a goal he couldn't pursue in Catholic-dominated Ireland—he left his family to go to America.

He arrived at the Ellis Island Immigration Center with only $5 in his pocket. His first project was to find a place to live. He was fortunate to locate a rooming house where he shared a room with a pharmacist who worked in a local drugstore.

Joseph's knowledge of English was minimal, as Gaelic was spoken both in his home and at school, so like most Irish immigrants, Joseph worked as a day laborer, earning enough to keep himself fed and housed.

He and his roommate became good friends, and when a job opened up at the drugstore where his friend worked, he was hired to be an assistant to the pharmacist. He immediately enrolled in a school to study pharmacy. With his keen mind and desire to learn, it didn't take long before Joseph passed the qualification exams and became a full-fledged pharmacist. He now made enough money to rent his own apartment. After a few years, he purchased the drugstore, and for the next few years ran a successful business.

When the United States entered World War II, Joseph enlisted in the Army and was assigned to work as a pharmacist in the medical unit of the 88th Infantry Division. At that time, he renewed his interest in religion and began to read extensively about various spiritual beliefs. After his discharge from the Army, he chose not to return to his career in pharmacy. He traveled extensively, taking courses in several universities both in the United States and abroad.

From his studies, Joseph became enraptured with the various Asian religions and went to India to learn about them in depth. He studied all of the major faiths and their histories. He extended these studies to the great philosophers from ancient times until the present.

Although he studied with some of the most intelligent and farsighted professors, the one person who most influenced Joseph was Dr. Thomas Troward, who was a judge as well as a philosopher, doctor, and professor. Judge Troward became Joseph's mentor and introduced him to the study of philosophy, theology, and law as well as mysticism and the Masonic order. Joseph became an active member of this order, and over the years rose in the Masonic ranks to the 32nd degree in the Scottish Rite.

Upon his return to the United States, Joseph chose to become a minister and bring his broad knowledge to the public. As his concept of Christianity was not traditional and indeed ran counter to most of the Christian denominations, he founded his own church in Los Angeles. He attracted a small number of congregants, but it did not take long for his message of optimism and hope rather than the "sin-and-damnation" sermons of so many ministers to attract many men and women to his church.

Dr. Joseph Murphy was a proponent of the New Thought movement. This movement was developed in the late 19th and early 20th centuries by many philosophers and deep thinkers who studied this phenomenon and preached, wrote, and practiced a new way of looking at life. By combining a metaphysical, spiritual, and pragmatic approach to the way we think and live, they uncovered the secret of attaining what we truly desire.

The proponents of the New Thought movement preached a new idea of life that is based on practical, spiritual principles that we can all use to enrich our lives and created perfected results. We can do these things only as we have found the law and worked out the understanding of the law, which God seems to have written in riddles in the past.

Of course, Dr. Murphy wasn't the only minister to preach this positive message. Several churches, whose ministers and congregants were influenced by the New Thought movement, were founded and developed in the decades following World War II. The Church of Religious Science, Unity Church, and other places of worship preach philosophies similar to this. Dr. Murphy named his organization The Church of Divine Science. He often shared platforms, conducted joint programs with his like-minded colleagues, and trained other men and women to join his ministry.

Over the years, other churches joined with him in developing an organization called the Federation of Divine Science, which serves as an umbrella for all Divine Science churches. Each of the Divine Science church leaders continues to push for more education, and Dr.

Murphy was one of the leaders who supported the creation of the Divine Science School in St. Louis, Missouri, to train new ministers and provide ongoing educational education for both ministers and congregants.

The annual meeting of the Divine Science ministers was a must to attend, and Dr. Murphy was a featured speaker at this event. He encouraged the participants to study and continue to learn, particularly about the importance of the subconscious mind.

Over the next few years, Murphy's local Church of Divine Science grew so large that his building was too small to hold them. He rented The Wilshire Ebell Theater, a former movie theater. His services were so well attended that even this venue could not always accommodate all who wished to attend. Classes conducted by Dr. Murphy and his staff supplemented his Sunday services that were attended by 1,300 to 1,500 people. Seminars and lectures were held most days and evenings. The church remained at the Wilshire Ebell Theater in Los Angeles until 1976, when it moved to a new location in Laguna Hills, California.

To reach the vast numbers of people who wanted to hear his message, Dr. Murphy also created a weekly radio talk show, which eventually reached an audience of over a million listeners. Many of his followers suggested that he tape his lectures and radio programs. He was at first reluctant to do so, but agreed to experiment. His radio programs were recorded on extra-large 78-rpm discs, a common practice at that time. He had six cassettes made from one of these discs and placed them on the information table in the lobby of the Wilshire Ebell Theater. They sold out the first hour. This started a new venture. His tapes of his lectures explaining biblical texts, and providing meditations and prayers for his listeners, were not only sold in his church, but in other churches and bookstores and via mail order.

As the church grew, Dr. Murphy added a staff of professional and administrative personnel to assist him in the many programs in which he was involved and in researching and preparing his first books. One of the most effective members of his staff was his administrative secretary, Dr. Jean Wright. Their working relationship developed into a romance, and they were married—a lifelong partnership that enriched both of their lives.

At this time (the 1950s), there were very few major publishers of spiritually inspired material. The Murphys located some small publishers in the Los Angeles area, and worked with them to produce a series of small books (often 30 to 50 pages printed in pamphlet form) that were sold, mostly in churches, from $1.50 to $3.00 per book. When the orders for these books increased to the point where they required second and third printings, major publishers recognized that there was a market for such books and added them to their catalogs.

Dr. Murphy became well known outside of the Los Angeles area as a result of his books, tapes, and radio broadcasts, and was invited to lecture all over the country. He did not limit his lectures to religious matters, but spoke on the historical values of life, the art of wholesome living, and the teachings of great philosophers— from both Eastern and Western cultures.

As Dr. Murphy never learned to drive, he had to arrange for somebody to drive him to the various places where he was invited to lecture in his very busy schedule. One of Jean's functions as his administrative secretary and later as his wife was to plan his assignments and arrange for trains or flights, airport pickups, hotel accommodations, and all the other details of the trips.

The Murphys traveled frequently to many countries around the world. One of his favorite working vacations was to hold seminars on cruise ships. These trips lasted a week or more and would take him to many countries around the world. In his lectures, he emphasized the importance of understanding the power of the subconscious mind and the life principles based on belief in the one God, the "I AM."

One of Dr. Murphy's most rewarding activities was speaking to the inmates at many prisons. Many ex-convicts wrote him over the years, telling him how his words had truly turned their lives around and inspired them to live spiritual and meaningful lives.

Dr. Murphy's pamphlet-sized books were so popular that he began to expand them into more detailed and longer works. His wife gave us some insight into his manner and method of writing. She reported that he wrote his manuscripts on a tablet and pressed so hard on his pencil or pen that you could read the imprint on the next page. He seemed to be in a trance while writing. He would remain in his office for four to six hours without disturbance until he stopped and said that was enough for the day. Each day was the same. He never went back into the office again until the next morning to finish what he'd started. He took no food or drink while he was working, He was just alone with his thoughts and his huge library of books, to which he referred from time to time. His wife sheltered him from visitors and calls and took care of church business and other activities.

Dr. Murphy was always looking for simple ways to discuss the issues and to elaborate points. He chose some of his lectures to present on cassettes, records, or CDs, as technologies developed in the audio field.

His entire collection of CDs and cassettes are tools that can be used for most problems that individuals encounter in life. His basic theme is that the solution to problems lies within you. Outside elements cannot change your thinking. That is, your mind is your own. To live a better life, it's your mind, not outside circumstances, that you must change. You create your own destiny. The power of change is in your mind, and by using the power of your subconscious mind, you can make changes for the better.

Dr. Murphy wrote more than 30 books. His most famous work, *The Power of the Unconscious Mind,* which was first published in 1963, became an immediate bestseller. It was acclaimed as one of the best self-help guides ever written. Millions of copies have been sold and continue to be sold all over the world.

Among some of his other best-selling books were *Telepsychics—The Magic Power of Perfect Living, The Amazing Laws of Cosmic Mind, Secrets of the I-Ching, The Miracle of Mind Dynamics, Your Infinite Power to Be Rich,* and *The Cosmic Power Within You.*

Dr. Murphy died in December 1981, and his wife, Dr. Jean Murphy, continued his ministry after his death. In a lecture she gave in 1986, quoting her late husband, she reiterated his philosophy:

> I want to teach men and women of their Divine Origin, and the powers regnant within them. I want to inform that this power is within and that they are their own saviors and capable of achieving their own salvation. This is the message of the Bible and nine-tenths of our confusion today is due to wrongful, literal interpretation of the life-transforming truths offered in it.
>
> I want to reach the majority, the man on the street, the woman overburdened with duty and suppression of her talents and abilities. I want to help others at every stage or level of consciousness to learn of the wonders within.

She said of her husband: "He was a practical mystic, possessed by the intellect of a scholar, the mind of a successful executive, the heart of the poet." His message summed up was: "You are the king, the ruler of your world, for you are one with God."

Hay House Titles of
Related Interest

Notes

Notes

Notes

Notes

Notes

Notes

Notes

Notes

Notes

Notes

Notes

Notes

Notes

Notes

Notes

Notes

We hope you enjoyed this Hay House book.
If you'd like to receive a free catalog featuring additional
Hay House books and products, or if you'd like information about the
Hay Foundation, please contact:

Hay House, Inc.
P.O. Box 5100
Carlsbad, CA 92018-5100

(760) 431-7695 or (800) 654-5126
(760) 431-6948 (fax) or (800) 650-5115 (fax)
www.hayhouse.com® • www.hayfoundation.org

Published and distributed in Australia by: Hay House Australia Pty. Ltd.,
18/36 Ralph St., Alexandria NSW 2015 • *Phone:*
612-9669-4299 • *Fax:* 612-9669-4144 • www.hayhouse.com.au

Published and distributed in the United Kingdom by: Hay House UK, Ltd.,
292B Kensal Rd., London W10 5BE • *Phone:* 44-20-8962-1230
Fax: 44-20-8962-1239 • www.hayhouse.co.uk

Published and distributed in the Republic of South Africa by: Hay House SA
(Pty), Ltd., P.O. Box 990, Witkoppen 2068 • *Phone/Fax:* 27-11-467-8904
orders@psdprom.co.za • www.hayhouse.co.za

Published in India by: Hay House Publishers India, Muskaan
Complex, Plot No. 3, B-2, Vasant Kunj, New Delhi 110 070
Phone: 91-11-4176-1620 • *Fax:* 91-11-4176-1630 • www.hayhouse.co.in

Distributed in Canada by: Raincoast, 9050 Shaughnessy St.,
Vancouver, B.C. V6P 6E5 • *Phone:* (604) 323-7100
Fax: (604) 323-2600 • www.raincoast.com

Tune in to **HayHouseRadio.com**® for the best in inspirational talk
radio featuring top Hay House authors! And, sign up via the Hay House
USA Website to receive the Hay House online newsletter and stay informed
about what's going on with your favorite authors. You'll receive bimonthly
announcements about: Discounts and Offers, Special Events, Product
Highlights, Free Excerpts, Giveaways, and more!
www.hayhouse.com®